MARGUERITE DURAS

Contributors:

Joël Farges
Francois Barat
Xavière Gauthier
Pierre Barat
Claire Devarrieux
Jacques Grant
Jacques Frenais
Jacques Lacan
Maurice Blanchot
Dionys Mascolo
Pierre Fédida
Benoît Jacquot
Viviane Forrester
Bernard Emmanuel Graciet
Jean-Louis Libois
Catherine Weinzaepflen

Translated by

Edith Cohen
Peter Connor

MARGUERITE DURAS

by
Marguerite Duras

City Lights Books
San Francisco

This book was originally published as *Marguerite Duras,* © 1976 by Albatros, Paris. A revised second edition was published in *Collection Ça/Cinema,* vol. 2, Albatros, in 1979.

Designed by Patricia Fujii

Library of Congress Cataloging-in-Publication Data

Duras, Marguerite.
  Marguerite Duras.

  Translation of Marguerite Duras.
  1. Duras, Marguerite—Interviews. 2. Authors,
French—20th century—Interviews. 3. Duras,
Marguerite—Criticism and interpretation. I. Cohen,
Edith. II. Title.
PQ2607.U8245Z46513   1987   843'.912   86-32702
ISBN 0-87286-198-8
ISBN 0-87286-199-6 (pbk.)

Many of these translations were made in collaboration with City Lights' editors Nancy J. Peters and Amy Scholder. Helpful suggestions were made by Denise Casabianca, Bill West, Lawrence Ferlinghetti, and Jason Ales.

CITY LIGHTS BOOKS are edited by Lawrence Ferlinghetti & Nancy J. Peters and published at the City Lights Bookstore, 261 Columbus Avenue, San Francisco, California 94133.

CONTENTS

INDIA SONG

Introduction
Joël Farges and François Barat

Undertaken while *India Song* was being shot, this compelling and necessary book is being distributed as Marguerite Duras begins another film, *Vera Baxter* ou *Les plages de l'Atlantique*. That is, this book followed step by step what we must now call the *India Song event*. First of all, there was the feverish and uncertain confidence in the shoot in which the participants, the witnesses, already saw how radically different this film was going to be.[1] Then came the first showings, when *India Song* challenged each of us in such a way, with such a rare and extreme violence, that the importance of this work was from then on luminously evident. Finally, there was its successful encounter with a public that had been revitalized and that grew larger week by week. A daily record could have been made of anecdotes, all the actions and reactions of the audience: the woman who entered at two, then refused to give up her seat for the evening show; the man who came back, apologizing for having left before the end and for having stepped out for a moment.

Not only, then, is the film *India Song* important, but also what it provokes, what it opens up in the way of new possibilities in the field of cinematography. All of a sudden a film emerged that no one could stop or block, a film that had to be considered original, sweeping aside what had for so long been made by force of habit. After *India Song* something else became possible in cinema, this still nameless cinema, something which cannot be named but which might be called, if you like, a "different cinema," a "young cinema."

India Song is a center, a place, a zone that illuminates every practice that claims to be new. From now on, we must go in that direction. Indeed, take a new path.

---

[1]The journal of the *India Song* filming was written by Nicole Lise Bernheim, "Marguerite Duras Tourne un Film," *Ca/Cinéma*.

1

India Song is not unique in Marguerite Duras's work; it follows upon consistent filmmaking. Before it, there was *Détruire, dit-elle, Jaune le soleil, Nathalie Granger,* and *La femme du Gange*—unbreakable links which lead to *India Song* but don't stop there, because with Marguerite Duras things are always taken up again.

For us, these films are unforgettable and, with some rare exceptions, undiscussed. It is a strange silence, all the more disturbing because unmotivated. We have to return to the period prior to *India Song,* not to discover an origin or a filiation from film to film (we can't; Marguerite Duras's work is made up of perpetual and unpredictable displacements, against a film, against a book . . .), but to affirm that these films have their own real importance which ought not to be hidden.

No doubt, there is in *India Song* a strange seduction, a disturbing fascination; but what is at issue in all these films? A provocation. A provocation of the subject in a place where the sealed, buried but steadfast beginning of a rebellious, analytic enterprise is discerned; it is a test of meaning, a disruption of structure, a crisis of the subject. A provocation which assumes the form of reversals which seem acute to western consciousness. (Thus, the woman is the reverse of custom, not an object of exchange but the regulator of exchange. Through her burning desire, ablaze and devouring, it is the woman who now regulates even the interiority of a film, the economic postures, the come-and-go for nothing of the exchange, etc.) New voices, indeed.

But this crisis is not isolated, it has repercussions in history (a date is specified for *India Song,* 1937); that is to say, it is linked to a political background. To restate what Sollers said, the question Marguerite Duras raises is that of "the possibility of articulating an analytic discourse and its exterior, political discourse; or, conversely, of articulating a political discourse with its analytic exterior."[2]

What to say? What to write? We can see that Marguerite Duras's work opens up infinite possibilities. To write what you

[2]"Détruire, dit-elle," Ph. Sollers, *Revue Ça/Cinéma,* no. 1.

want, this is the paradoxical invitation. Her texts, films, can in no way be examined or reasoned because they resonate elsewhere, in a logic alien to the empire of knowledge.

These films and texts—inalienable, luminous and impenetrable—return the reader to his original position, to his value-making function: that of a new stance for writing.

Not mastery, but a sudden effacement (once writing has taken place) confronts us.

PATHS

This is important: Marguerite Duras shapes the very terms of cinema to her desire. Each time, the film is an experiment. Experimenting with voices, innovation in its open-centered perspective, complex gaps between images and sound, etc.—all this transforms filmmaking. Thus, this *"film of voices"* which reverberates, collides with and dissects itself, is divided so that it draws on an extraordinary reserve of inexhaustible meaning. Essential discoveries generating new possibilities in writing.

The entire production of the film participates in this refusal, this hostility, this disgust with cinematic spectacle. Naturalism (stupid representation) is destroyed. Perspective, equivocal positioning of actors, the sets' appearance, rigorously immobile shots, effects of seeing—all this moves the cinema toward a strange figuration where representation is exchanged for another, enigmatic, language.

What image do we have of *India Song?* What do we see in it?

The image of what body rushes by and flees into the mirror? Going where? Beyond the frame? Who returns in this mirror-hole with its virtual, false, true, and oblique images that shut off representation as one stops a hemorrhage?

We make every effort to see into *India Song;* but finally what was aimed at—"the threshold of the interval between deaths"— can only be glimpsed. We hear them behind us, invoke and evoke them, without meeting a living soul; so is it true, then, that the gaze cannot be returned? That this film is invisible?

With *La femme du Gange* and *India Song,* fictional narrative culminates and sharply exceeds the cinematic apparatus. These bodies, through the effects of exacerbated phantomization (escaped

3

from death just in time)—what are they? People? Entirely dead? Alive? This knowledge is of no importance in the end. They are afflicted, it is certain. But by what? Leprosy?

Phantoms of phantoms, these bodies—in the precarious position of characters—have no origin and yet have memories, but to whom do they belong? And (in what state?) are they the wreckage of a knowledge destroyed? A destruction that continually returns, a watchword that returns to the present. Echo-witness of a wound scarcely healed, like the essence or the heart of an unknown, unfindable, and obscure wound.

The cinema-machine is disturbed to the point where *India Song* cannot be seen to adhere to or participate in what is happening. *India Song* touches us elsewhere; at the highest point it captures us through the unknown, or by something *known*, which escapes us while we scarcely escape from it.

LOVE

The avant-garde in recent times has had no love story. What Marguerite Duras brings to the surface is passion. Can desire be allowed to rove free as the winds? It's destructive, of course, because it's scandalous, excessive, "emotive," in some way obscene. Isn't the body (of the actor, the character, the viewer) utterly carried away, perturbed, exalted, deranged?

Passion for love, because finally it's love we are in love with. Doesn't the love object disappear, isn't it cancelled out under the weight of love?

This utopia of the horde, in which it is not the father who is to be consumed, but something else; this communal dream *loves.* Desire lurks in it, weaving its way through many snares and spinning out its tragic impossibility.

Thus, the cry of the Vice-Consul. Before him, who would have been able to cry out like that? The culminating moment of the film—obscene because unbearable and real—creates a scandal; it's base to cry out, a cry connected to acts of senseless violence and cruelty, and to the surrounding madness. This cry, which leaves the body completely disorganized, leads us straight back to the sacred, that object of horror and desire. What would we hear if it could be listened to? The madness of a body? The shudder of or-

4

gans? Is it audible when, from the omnipotence of the organs, someone cries out this way at love?

Let's risk this last proposition: it might be that *India Song* is the most beautiful contemporary film. But let's wait for *Vera Baxter*, before deciding definitely.

Introduction to the first edition
October 1975

5

SINGULAR

Introduction
Joël Farges

We knew from the first edition of this book that with *India Song* something was in the wind for contemporary filmmaking. Something had happened, something like a crisis in Western representation as it was taken over by the cinematographic system. We felt, in a confused way, that a unique and irreversible experiment had taken place. We never completely recovered from that experiment. Dionys Mascolo spoke admirably of *India Song* as a "birth in Tragedy," and he was right.

We came away impressed by this film. Impressed in a photographic sense, as in Hiroshima, where we see (in a terrifying image in photographic negative) the shadowy trace of a sentry burned alive, imprinted forever in the calcinated blackness of a brick wall.

India Song crossed over a boundary and penetrated other regions, the extent of which each essay in this book tries to demonstrate.

The four films that followed (we focused on them as closely as possible—François Barat was the producer of two of them) did not fail to meet our expectations.

Marguerite Duras didn't disappoint us. She followed the path she had marked out for herself. A path all the more unique and rigorous in that it was paved with re-evaluation, with obliteration and rearrangement of earlier work.

I shall insist that her path is all the more rare in the sad, dispirited period in which we find ourselves, in that she is very much alone, no doubt the only one who has drawn from herself such matchless strength, and has blazed such a trail.

Destroying the range of certainties that underlie filmmaking, she challenges the purpose and effect of cinema in her own way and shapes them to her desire. Each film in differing degree is an experiment in courage, a return to "point zero" of an invention which is, after all, a recent one. See *Son nom de Venise; India Song* is swept aside, suddenly she is not happy with it, it isn't enough, she starts all over again.

And with this fresh start, Marguerite Duras once again becomes aware of the impossibility (the imbecility?) of making films. To what end?

Tenaciously, she makes a film about this impossibility itself, *Le Camion*. Suspended above an abyss—is it a film? Is it only a project? The gap between the two? A hesitation between the one and the other?

Expérience des limites: experiencing and experimenting with limits—never has such an expression been more appropriate. In other words, it means an apprenticeship of no return. Each film is a test, a journey from which there is no turning back.

But where does this strength come from, the energy to go on like this from film to film? I think she feels the constant peril of death. This sense of peril does not come from fear of an imminent catastrophe, nor from a certain recurring, painful memory. It comes from forgetting, from tensions between death and life, from a lucidity about the mortal condition. This danger tells us that life ruins life, that the first desire brings on the first death . . . .

Two other bodies of work (two equally awesome experiments) are commensurate with those of Marguerite Duras: those of Goya and Pascal.

She would like to have made a film which brought together both the painter and the writer. Perhaps she will do it . . . .

But think of this: the mad woman of Gouchy, the beggar woman of Savannakhet, the shorn woman of Hiroshima: Goya.

The lucid, almost mathematical writing of tragic clairvoyance: Pascal.

The dialectic of the two: Duras.

Introduction to the second edition
December 1978

7

I make films to occupy my time. If I were strong enough to do nothing, I wouldn't do anything at all. It's because I'm not strong enough to do nothing that I make films. There isn't any other reason. There is nothing truer I can say about my enterprise.

Marguerite Duras

NOTES ON INDIA SONG

Introduction
Marguerite Duras

I am publishing the shooting script of the first part of *India Song* without the dialogue for the *Voices* that corresponds to the shots. Of course, only those who have seen this film and who want to *re-view* it will read this script. It seems to me that a simultaneous reading of image and sound might impede the film's continuity and its agenda. Then, too, the texts spoken by the *Voices* in this first part are the same as those in the book, and can be found there. This is not true for those in the second part, which are set down differently than they are in the book and are very often original.

We worked and shot the film from this shooting script. The manuscript itself was duplicated and distributed. As you can see, it doesn't include any technical directions. Some people will find it too vague and also too "written." I have never been able to write a purely technical script. I always write for members of the crew, who are *readers*. Why should the very meaning of my project be inaccessible to them? Why block their integration into the film? What's more, it seems to me that technique is always the least useful element to write down. It *is* the shot itself at the moment it's conceived. The size, the light, the framing of a shot—*that's* the shot. Inevitably, the director comes to the shooting with a mental script of the film. As perfect and exact as a technical shooting script may be, it can never *translate what one is seeing* by itself. Only the meaning of the whole project, with each shot and the memory of it—indicating how the fragment is related to the whole, *is* the whole—can begin to bring about this translation. Technique as such can only become the secondary translation of the meaning, and most often it will take care of itself.

During the rehearsals of *India Song*, the lines spoken by the *Voices* and the guests, as well as the text describing the shot itself ("he enters, he looks, he would like to see her . . .") were read aloud and recorded. When necessary, a second tape recorder took over the music, and during the shooting this oral scenario was developed completely.

The shots were lengthy and so of course we had to monitor the placement of speech within them. But this had to be done for other reasons too; on one hand, so that the actors (and camera) would understand the meaning of these shots at the moment they were supposed to make that meaning appear and express it; and, on the other hand, so that the meaning would emerge and be expressed at the same time, *outside of them*. It would be done *there*, expressed *there*, and said *here*. So that the expression would escape them in part. If it said in the oral scenario, for example, "A.M. Stretter enters the private salon, looks at the park," Delphine Seyrig actually entered, looked at the park. *But at the same time, she listened to them say she was doing it*. So, when she entered, she entered *less*, looked at the park *less*, and in contrast listened *more*. The words describing what she was doing were meant to express this *lessness* of her entrance and her looking at the same time she did. This speaking, this oral scenario, was to disappear during the editing process, leaving Delphine alone to make an entrance and look at the park. And yet, Delphine's distraction, caused by what she heard, is in the film. I think that in *India Song* it is only this distraction, this subordination to speech, that could be called *understanding the meaning*. Because Delphine heard a voice say that at that moment *a woman entered and looked at the park, but not she in particular*, and only the medium of speech led her to feel and express the *generality of the expression* "a woman."

When I say meaning, I mean speech. When I say listening to the meaning, I mean listening to speech. And understanding the meaning, an irreducibility, yet one to which we must constantly adhere.

When I speak of the *meaning* of a shot, I refer to the *direction* it takes, what gives it over to the next shot and what it takes in its turn when it is surpassed. Nothing else. The general meaning of a film, I believe, is both the permanence of this direction and the flow of different intensities as it moves through the shots. And certainly, too, the implementation of its ending: to stop the current *here*, in the film, but not to let it dry up *there*, once the film has ended; no, *to give it back to the world*. A river that one would gather in and then give back to the waters of the world. And this *giving back* should be seen, should be read *in* the film. Let Calcutta come out of its dwelling place, and then take its place outside of the film, on the outside. In the same way as death, as silence.

How the crew listens to the meaning has no doubt given the film (more than all of the author's technical directions) its own pace, unity of movement and light, its own breath and body. It has made all the actors flow toward and become wedded to this body. I saw all *India Song's* actors develop the *same temperament* during the shooting—distanced from themselves in the same way, all in retreat, humble with like humility. As if they were all equally determined to listen to what they would be asked to express, were it possible to express it, somewhere other than where they were, in an ideal place where meaning would be reducible, for example, to the performance. Or, if you like, in an ideal place of speech, still scarcely glimpsed—in cinema.

I see them, yes, as absent, therefore, restored to themselves in this film, cleansed of a self-esteem that usually conceals the star's performance and deprives the viewer of seeing beyond the performer to his function. I see their absence as parallel to our own when we watch them in the film, and when, having gone astray, we meet up with one another.

I think that this strange, very vital and enduring tenderness that binds me to these actors who played in *India Song* must stand out, along with the selflessness of their performance.

Of the second part of *India Song*, the reception at the French Embassy, I will publish only the script and dialogues without the shooting script that belongs to them. The opposite of what I did with the first part. Except for two shots—since I have been asked—to use as an example, so as to compare the first and last shooting scripts: the one that was for the most part filmed, and the old one; so an opinion can be formed about the cuts made over the time (and, I believe, only over time) that separates the project from its shooting.

11

The reception lasts more than an hour (sixty-six minutes and thirteen seconds). I see it all as a resonant mass which revolves around scarcely changing images, more or less fixed supports that anchor this mass in position, preventing it from drifting off toward illustration. The development of the narrative no longer follows episodes, chronologies of space and time. I see it as the only event, one of unique content, isolated in the film. Here, time passes, and time alone. The sixty-six minutes that the reception lasts represent five or six hours of the reception's duration—between the first hours of the night and dawn—while the twenty-nine minutes of the first part represent several weeks, or several months, of Anne-Marie Stretter's last days.

It is, then, the sound in this second part which will serve as a reminder for people who want to "re-view" *India Song*. I indicate with sound, that is, speech and music welded together, the dance through which the script unfolds.

Everything that is *unseen* in the reception has been planned, envisioned, and specified. Every exit, each entrance of the five people who alone "make" this reception, is motivated and accounted for. First, everything had to be logical and realistic before breaking loose, and the apparent disorder of the evening should never seem forced. On the contrary, everything was to be as clear as if the reception had been filmed in its entirety. When, for example, the Vice-Consul enters the private sitting room, it is because he is looking for Mme. Stretter, and if he searches for her there it's because in the preceding shot she was going in that direction, and so that must be where she is.

To speak about the reception in *India Song* is to inhibit the rapture I feel when I speak about it.

What one wants to keep from the reception scene, to extract from it, is the pursuit of Anne-Marie Stretter, the way she is hunted down by death, by the Vice-Consul from Lahore, the bearer of the feminine. It was supposed to end in a final rapprochement between him and her at the end of the night, with the fatally convincing expression of a shared understanding of the *refusal*. To end, therefore, with the final suicide. This refusal of life in the name of life extends even to love itself, and to the diversions of its articulation. ("Love affairs, you have with others, we don't need that," says the Vice-Consul. "We have nothing to say to each other, we are the same.") So amidst the swarms and profusions at the reception, this pursuit should never be lost from sight; it ought to be inscribed with the greatest clarity amid apparent disorder, never drowned out by secondary vicissitudes. To try to get this result, it was decided that the whole reception should take place in a single area we called "the rectangle," that is, the rectangular space of the private sitting room facing the mirror, as well as its reflected double. A double rectangle filmed along two axes, one extending to the gates of the park, out of vision for those at the reception, and the other formed by the walls of the apartments, never entered (except, it's true, for the two shots filmed in the Chinese drawing room on the second floor). This double rectangle contained the epicenter of the whole film, the photograph on the piano of the dead woman, Anne-Marie Stretter, with roses and incense in her memory—the altar. It should always fill the space, obstruct and constrict it, and, of course, cast doubt on all that happened in the rectangle and around it. The film was shot and made possible because that woman's story was stopped by death; the altar is a constant reminder of this. It was *also* because of pain, my pain. It welled up from this source.

Through this place where doubt is cast—the almost unchanging image of the rectangle—pass the five people assigned "to make" the reception, the murmurs of others, the music, guests' voices, dancing, conversations, the shouts of the madman from Lahore. In this interior place they tell the story in the present tense ("he *looks*," "they *dance*," "he *advances* toward . . ."). Whereas, in the places I have called *les bis des plans intérieurs*— moving lightly over the ruined facades of the Palais Rothschild— they speak in the past tense ("they *had* always talked about her," "she *would have* played music behind the walls . . ."). The interior place is crowded regularly with people passing through, and is emptied just as regularly, becoming once again the space for the altar, for the death that is contingent to the place, a recent death— the flowers are changed and someone comes to light the incense. Whereas, in *les bis des plans intérieurs* (with the exception of the

13

tennis courts), no one passes through anymore, not even the actors—they are uninhabitable, uninhabited, emptied once and for all by time—for everything is swallowed up by death.

The exterior shots also present a scarcely changing image, always immersed in night. Here, the surface of the image is Viviane Forrester's voice; it casts over the Rothschild facade a slow-paced narration of stories about the reception that everyone has just left, and about this woman's Calcutta. From *an earlier time, now that something can be said about it.*

It was between the two shooting scripts—the one from April and the one from June, 197—, that we decided to eliminate the extras at the reception. Following that, the characters George Crawn and the ambassador (the husband) were discarded. George Crawn appears once more, much later, at dawn; the ambassador, never again. The last one to be cut was The Woman in Black.[1] Nickie de Saint-Phalle refused to play this role; she was replaced by three photographs of the same woman done by Edouard Boubat after the war.[2]

Once the decision was made, it was inconceivable that we go back. All the characters that were cut became superfluous. If they had been restored to the film, they would have encumbered it, and this time it would have been artificially cumbersome. We found that what seemed in the beginning a matter of course stemmed only from habit and idiosyncrasy, and the extras' only function would have been to fill space—which one wanted free—and to delude people into believing in the reality of Calcutta and Lahore—*whereas it was she, this woman from Venice, and he, the Vice-Consul,* who *were Calcutta and Lahore.* To bring in two or ten other characters would be to rob them of their essential function, so that what was not indispensable became useless immediately, hence false.

She is Calcutta. Yes. In her is the rambling of the beggar woman, the song of Laos that passes through her. There is also the slowly rotating fan, the sweat on her naked body, the birds and the

---

[1]The Woman in Black was both a photograph and a woman. In the first part *her photograph* played a role (from the beginning). In the reception *people saw her* appear, alone, and look around. She was never seen.

[2]Two of which appeared in Edouard Boubat's album, *Femmes*, Ed. du Chêne, 1972.

dogs. Nothing else, I think. He alone is Lahore. We see nothing of Lahore but him.

Yes, these extras were supposed to reveal what was not seen of *Lahore:* the balcony overlooking the Shalimar gardens, the beggar woman, the faceless guests. *The voices were enough.* Only the indispensable was supposed to remain in the image: she, Anne-Marie Stretter; he, the Vice-Consul of Lahore; her other lover, Michael Richardson; and those two young men, the Young Attaché and the Young Guest; in other words, the *witnesses, us. Like us,* these two have no connection to her, neither in the present nor the past. Like us, they are not informed and must discover this story; or, rather, they look at it, they follow it with their eyes.

I tried to clear the space so that the geometry of the pursuit I've described above might be nakedly inscribed in it, so that is all we see. To work in such a way that the viewer will have nothing else to look at, will see *only that,* so that if he refuses to see it, it would be a complete, flawless refusal, and would have a bearing *on the film itself.* I am certain that *if one flees, one can only flee everything.* I avoided "catching up" scenes like a filmmaker's plague. No, one cannot mix genres. Even with the past behind us, it is difficult to extract, to depopulate, to tear down. Progress is made when one succeeds in doing these things. If I didn't believe one could sometimes succeed, I would never work in film again.

I wrote somewhere in my working notes before shooting: "*India Song will be built first through sound, then through light.*" And so, from the beginning I was already on the way to the final depopulation.

After the extras were removed and the space cleared, there still remained the problem of speech for the "five people." I wanted the two long conversations between Anne-Marie Stretter and the Young Attaché on the one hand, and between her and the Vice-Consul on the other, to be *seen* in the rectangle. I wanted people to see their bodies coming together, and that could only be seen when they danced and spoke in our presence (whereas in the book, these dances and conversations are off-screen). At the same time, I could not allow these conversations to work against the fundamental way the film casts doubt. Never was it necessary to

15

"relive" the story, nor to bring about, even for a few minutes, an identification between those people on the screen, *those actors*, and the *other people of Calcutta.* What was supposed to have been said by those people in these conversations had to be *said again*, but in the presence of a concrete sign of their death—in the same way as what was seen had to be seen in the presence of the dead woman's photograph. And, I discovered the *closed mouths:* although they speak, their mouths are silent.

Once this decision was made, like the one about the extras, there was no going back. They listen to their own voices, but without pronouncing the words, without actually speaking.

India Song is perhaps, yes, this: the bringing to ruin of any kind of reconstitution. If *India Song* is successful in any way, it can only be in that it documents a failed project. A result that fills me with hope. What can be called tragic here is not the tenor of the story it tells, nor the genre in which it falls according to traditional classification. Quite the opposite. It is the way the story is told that can be called tragic, that is to say, *in the bringing together and setting in relation* of *both* the story's destruction through death and forgetting *and* the love which it nevertheless continues to bring forth in abundance, even though it is destroyed. As if the only memory of this story was this love that flows from a bloodless body, a body riddled with holes. The terrain of the story is this contradiction, this laceration. The only possible setting for the story is the incessant swing of our despair *between this love and its body:* the very obstacle to any *narration.*

One last remark: there is no figure of the fool who talks about her, about Calcutta, no one who mocks. Why? It was as useless as piling up extras on the set. There are only those who think they are informed and who in turn become informed, and those who think they are informed and actually do know something. *But everyone knows they don't know everything.* It is with this baggage of fragmentary knowledge, and in an essential and permanent fear of untruthfulness, that I have tried to trace the ideas filmed in *India Song.*

INDIA SONG

Shooting Script

REEL I (15 shots) 15'12"

SHOT 1 Ext. STATIONARY SHOT. Evening (Shots 1 through 5 were filmed at the same time)

> Dusk over a valley.
> Red sun. (heat)
> The forest.
> It's deserted.

Silence

> Then, the ramblings and cries of the beggar woman very close by.
> Then, silence again.
> Then, the trace of a cry.
> Then silence.
> Then voices.

SHOT 2 id. 15 minutes later

> The beggar woman enters immediately, as if she caused the shot to change.
> She is less close.
> Shorter silence.
> The sun is less high,
> the colors darken,
> Always the ravine, wild.
> After the silence,

Voices

SHOT 3 id. 15 minutes later

> The night begins to fade.
> Silence.
> This time, it is the voices that begin.

Voices

> Then, the beggar woman.
> She laughs and cries, in the distance.

17

Then, silence.

SHOT 4 id. 15 minutes later

The sun has sunk halfway.

It's almost dark.

Silence.

Then, voices.

Then, silence.

Then, very far off, the beggar woman.

She sings. It fades away.

Silence.

Voices begin again.

Silence.

Cries of the beggar woman, very far off. She cries out the word "Savannakhet."

Goes away. Disappears.

Silence.

Then voices begin again immediately (the text on the beggar woman's childhood).

Then, silence.

Then, song of the beggar woman.

Traces of a song interrupted by a cry.

Then, silence.

SHOTS 5 id. But much later, almost dark

Silence.

Voices (that say "they were in Calcutta during the same years").

Then, "India Song" piano, for a long time.

SHOT 6 Very slow pan

On the floor (sofa) are fallen dresses: 2 to 3 dresses that we will not see in the film. And the red dress from the reception. Scarves. Dust. A fan. A powder box. A mirror. Necklaces, gloves.

> "India Song" piano
> (no text)

SHOT 7 Very slow pan

A series: Chinese drawing room and boudoir, Chinese

18

embroideries, bearskins.

On the floor, signs of life, incense burning.

Far off on the piano console, the photograph (of the dead woman) and roses (indecipherable), always fresh. "India Song."

SHOT 8

Repeat of 91² and 91³ of *La femme du Gange.*

(The table with scarves and overturned flowers.)

"India Song" far off.

Voices.

Then silence.

SHOT 9 STATIONARY SHOT (never shot)

Balcony corridor above an empty space.

Silence.

Then, voices.

SHOT 10 STATIONARY SHOT (In the editing this shot was part of reel 5)

The piano with the score of "India Song."

no text, no music

SHOT 11 Trav. (not used)

1. The photograph of "the dead woman, Anne-Marie Stretter"—fresh roses. Pull back to include the roses. (*Note:* the angle of filming should be the same in the next shot with the mirror.) Incense smoke between photograph and camera.

2. Or: sweep over to pan the photograph and the roses. Stop on the roses. Behind them, incense smoke.

no text, no music

SHOT 12 Int. Evening. The private drawing room

The mirror, framed like the photograph, id. angle.

Incense in the empty room

(incense: the link between the images of Calcutta).

Long silence.

One after another, the sounds, the murmurs of Calcutta (three minutes) are heard.

Low light.

Voices (that say they were dancing).

Then, following a reverse chronology:

"India Song" piano, savagely, after the remarks about the dance.

The camera pivots very slowly. And they appear (so they are there, very close to us) (sentence from the book: "there were people").

We see them, but in the mirror.

At first, Michael Richardson and Anne-Marie Stretter. They are embracing, motionless.

Then, the Young Guest. He leans against the piano, looking at the lovers.

Or:

The Young Guest appears first and then the lovers appear in the mirror (the solution that was kept).

The music dies down.

Disappears.

The sounds of Calcutta die down gradually.

Note: The light is very somber. Only the gaze of the Young Guest is illuminated, but scarcely so; he is the center of the image, its focus: *the one who looks.*

Voices

Then silence again, for a long time.

Then *rain.* Hard, and for a long time.

Rain.

The rain lets up.

Reverse process: the light returns.

And the sounds of Calcutta.

The couple separates and turns toward the outside. The Young Guest turns at the same time the couple does and, because of this, he is no longer in the light.

The three of them, a somber group, look at the rain.

We hear the joyful song of the beggar woman, we let it drift away.

Then silence.

Then Voices.

Then silence.

Then the cry of the beggar woman: "Savannakhet!"

SHOT 13 Palais Rothschild (discarded)

Anne-Marie Stretter in the mirror. She pronounces the word "Savannakhet": we see her pronounce the word silently, we don't hear it.

She looks at herself (discarded).

SHOT 14 (discarded)

The three of them look at the rain. Straight on.

Note: Here, the "discontinuity" will manifest itself in this way: we expect them to be looking toward the rain and we see them looking at nothing.

> Voices (text disconnected from all context, and therefore belonging to every context)

Note: Meaning of the 14th shot: "they were neither gay nor sad, they were not there, but elsewhere, *where there is no suffering.*"

SHOT 15

The three, from behind. They leave.

We stay there, in the empty room

(we see the wet terrace).

Outside: cries in Hindi in the distance.

> distant murmurs

Here: silence for a long time

(shot and cut during the editing).

Then, something like the sound of weeping.

And like a white shadow that passes slowly

along the terrace. Someone is there. We didn't see him.

He looks through the doors, disappears immediately.

Do we hear the man's footsteps? I don't know.

The weeping grows fainter.

He moves farther away. We don't know who he is.

We don't move. We don't try to see.

No text.

Perhaps "India Song" at the end of the shot, very low.

Or: the song of the beggar woman, far away.

SHOT 16 Evening. Palais Rothschild, pond
The man's white shadow reflected in the water of the pond.
Stopped there.
A man who looks.
Sound of weeping.
Voices (which identify the shadow: the Vice-Consul of
France in Lahore).

SHOT 17 Idem. Esplanade. Evening
On the esplanade, the three come toward us. Slow walk.
Commanding. (She wears a 1930s beret and a long scarf.)
Note: Here is the crumbled facade of the Palais Rothschild
and the commanding walk that effected the
"discontinuity."
They leave the shot.

SHOT 18 Idem. Pond
The white shadow, from the back (motionless), he looks at
them and turns around to follow with his eyes.
And leaves again.

SHOT 19 Idem. Flight of stairs, Palais Rothschild (cut into two shots)
The three.
They come closer. Descend the big stairway which leads to
the park.
Over the empty set, after their departure (camera left),
the ramblings of the beggar woman who comes closer.
Closer still.
Becomes completely present.
And his shadow appears, advances, stops advancing,
stands still.
The ramblings have also ceased.
(Shadow of the man who passed in front of the post office,
in Hiroshima, *photographed* in stone.)
First, the shadow is motionless.
Withdraws.
Then, the singing resumes.

Becomes faint.

SHOT 20 Evening. Tennis Courts

The tennis courts. Anne-Marie Stretter's red bicycle against the fence.

The song of the beggar woman continues. Then is cut off.

The white shadow comes into view.

Seen from the back, it stops. Looks.

Goes away.

Disappears.

After its disappearance, *Voices.*

Hold camera on the empty set.

The beggar woman, still.

SHOT 18b Evening. Rothschild Park (not planned for in the shooting script)

The Vice-Consul on a path in the Japanese garden in the Rothschild Park.

He stops. Is still looking.

REEL II (10 SHOTS) 14'23"

SHOT 21 Evening. Private sitting room

The Indian servant lights the lamps, lights the incense.

Arranges the roses near the photograph of the dead woman.

The singing of the beggar woman (which continues) is the link between time and place.

Two bursts of fire (cut in the editing).

Two lights dim suddenly.

The servant stands still, waits for the singing of the beggar woman to resume.

The beggar woman's singing and light return.

Voices.

The servant moves, continues on, he lights the lamps (around the mirror).

Slows down.

He leaves.

Voices (slow) over the empty set.
Silence.
Nothing. Nothing happens.
Then, *voices*.
Then silence.
Still nothing.
Then, *voices*.
Then silence again.
Then, voices again.
Then silence.
Then Anne-Marie Stretter enters.
Hair in disarray.
Dressed in the black peignoir of the dead woman.
She goes toward the doors leading to the park, stays there.
Murmuring sounds of Calcutta.
Then, at the end of the shot, she turns around like someone
who feels herself watched, toward the photograph of the
dead woman.
And she approaches the photograph.
Looks at it.

SHOT 23 (in fact, a continuation of shot 21)
Anne-Marie Stretter in front of the photograph.
From a distance, she looks at it, her back to the piano.
We see the two of them: the photograph (of the
dead woman, and the profile of the living woman).
Then she leaves the shot.
The camera remains on the photograph without moving.
Silence.
Then, *Voices*.
Then a long silence.

SHOT 23
On the rug, lying in a foetal position; as if clutching
the floor, shrunken, a black pool, her face invisible:
Anne-Marie Stretter.
Voices (talking about her).
While the *voices* speak, Michael Richardson enters by the

"secret door" and looks at her until the voices stop.[1]

Silence.

He moves next to her, sits down.

Then, he gently turns her over. She appears naked under her peignoir. Violence in his gesture of touching the body as it's turned. He caresses her forehead, wipes away the tears, the sweat.

(Takes her hands, looks at them, lets them go.)

(They fall back, dead.)

He lies down, head in his hands.

Voices.

Voices again.

Meanwhile, the Young Guest enters through the secret door.

At first he goes toward the park.

Gesture indicating heat.

Then he comes back to sit next to the pair who are lying down.

He is still in the most brightly lit area of the set. This time he doesn't look at them.

Voices, for a long time (indifferent to the image).

The young guest lies down in turn.

Voices.

Then the lover stretches out more completely, in a sleeping position.

DARK SHOT - THREE IMAGES COLORED BLACK (discarded)

SHOT 24 (in fact following shot 23)

What did the girl from S. Thala want?

"To see them," say the *Voices.*

We see them: we are closer to them.

The lover's hand still caresses her.

Silence.

Then, noises from the Ganges, oars, water stirred.

Then laughter in the distance (cry of the beggar woman).

---

[1]An intermediate shot was filmed: the peignoir and Anne-Marie Stretter's brownish-red wig, detached from the body, like the dresses in shot 6.

Then merchants' calls.

Then nothing more.

Eight seconds of silence *before* the Voices.

Then, Voices interrupted by silence.

Eight seconds of silence *after* the Voices.

Michael Richardson's hand is stopped during this silence.

Very somber light.

The hand begins to caress the naked body again.

Rain.

Voices.

Eight seconds of silence again.

Then the first question bursts forth from the *Voices*
about the past in Venice:

Voice of the question that was asked ("Was she from
Venice?").

And at the same time, Beethoven's 14th Variation on a
Waltz of Diabelli starts up (the music: Venice).

BLACK SHOT 3 BLACK-COLORED IMAGES (discarded)

SHOT 25 (discarded)

The gaze of the two men at Anne-Marie Stretter's naked
body.

The intensity of the 14th Variation has diminished.

Anne-Marie Stretter's body is in the shadow.

*The gazes of the two are lit (very faintly) as they look at the
dark body.*

We wait several seconds before the answer to the question
asked in shot 24.

(*Note:* Deliberate disjunction of time between question and
answer. Here, the image waits for the text.)

The two men are listening to the 14th Variation.

The voices too.

Everything, everyone waits until the music fades in volume.

It grows fainter little by little.

Here, it is possible *to hear* the answer above the faint music:
then the voices answer. ("Yes. Her music, it was in
Venice . . . .")

Silence.

Then voices continue, always about Venice.

SHOT OF THE INSERTS OF PHOTO ALBUMS OF LAOS
(discarded)

SHOT 26

We no longer see the men. Camera on Anne-Marie Stretter's body beneath her breasts, under the rib cage. *We see her breathing.* (Her hand, resting on her breast, rises and falls.)

Note: Her breathing is enclosed in the cage of her body like her body was once caged in Laos, within the fences of the General Administration.

Silence.

Then *Voices.*

The body stirs suddenly.

The voices stop. *Wait until the body regains its calm, its tranquility.*

Then, begin narrating again.

After the sentence: "Take her away from Savannakhet," the beggar woman's cry in the night takes up this word and she cries it out: Savannakhet! A strange summons, as if the beggar woman had *also* heard the *Voices* say this word.

The beggar woman is gone.

Voices, still.

Then silence.

SHOT 29 Frame of the door opening onto the park. View of the Vice-Consul

They sleep as if prostrated by the heat, as if dead.

Silence.

(We should have the feeling that someone else besides ourselves is looking at them—shadow of the Vice-Consul? Should the park be better lit?)

The *Voices* have seen nothing, continue to narrate.

SHOT 28 Close-up of the Vice-Consul

The Vice-Consul looks at her savagely for the first time. (His eyes seem almost to burst with the power of their gaze at her.)

27

The voices speak of Anne-Marie Stretter's "splendor" and say the word "love."
At this point the text becomes the Vice-Consul's.
Silence.
The Vice-Consul leaves.
After his exit, several seconds later, the three bodies move together as a group: she rises and looks ahead—toward the Vice-Consul who disappears.
She looks (a dull, inexpressive look).
Then, she lies down again.
Silence. Motionless.
Then, Michael Richardson's hand caresses Anne-Marie Stretter's hair once more. So, he was not asleep.
The last movement dies out in turn.
The light fades inside.
It gets brighter outside.
(Cries of the Vice-Consul. For a long time.)
Then, silence.
Voices (that speak of the crematoriums of Calcutta).
Unnoticed, a servant passes by and turns off the lights that he had lit, one after the other, as if after a performance.
14th Variation.
Wan light on the bodies that sleep.
Silence.

SHOT 20 (what Anne-Marie Stretter looks at)
The Vice-Consul embraces Anne-Marie Stretter's bicycle, this "thing that she has touched."
Sound of weeping.
No text.
Stays leaning against the bicycle.
Then turns around.
And looks, looks at it.
And leaves.
Empty set.

SHOT 31 C.U. A.M.S. (discarded)

SHOT 32 C.U. V.C. (discarded)

SHOT 33 M.C.S. in which Michael Richardson looks at Anne-Marie Stretter (discarded)

SHOT 34 to follow shot 29 (discarded)

A photograph on the piano of the dead woman, Anne-Marie Stretter; rectangular, approached at a slant. The roses are in the foreground and conceal the photograph almost completely.

The *Voices* (speak about the crime in Lahore).

The sun reaches the piano, pale. What appears in the photograph is unfamiliar: we don't recognize it.

SHOT 35 (discarded)

We get closer to the photograph. We have gone around the roses. We still don't recognize it.

The Vice-Consul weeping in the distance.

Then, the beggar woman laughing.

The *Voices* continue to tell about the crime in Lahore.

The sun fades from the piano.

The first Voice asks: "He couldn't bear India?"

"No." "What about India?"

We stop with that question.

SHOT 36 (discarded)

The photograph fills the screen. And always, the roses.

It is the photograph of Anne-Marie Stretter, young, seen in profile, dazzling.

The second voice responds to the question: "The idea."

Silence.

End of the First Part

SHOOTING SCRIPT FROM APRIL 15, 1974

NOTE I:

In order for I and II to mesh, the method of filming must be the same. No dispersion. Never move away from the axis of the film;

29

an idea ought not to define this, but only a word: *penetration* (of what is impenetrable). A given place is penetrated, *the place of a woman, Anne-Marie Stretter.*

The word is not used frivolously here: *one penetrates what ordinarily cannot be penetrated, the inexhaustible writing about Anne-Marie Stretter.*

The Pommereux hotel lacks magic. It is a flat place. What contains Anne-Marie Stretter is therefore flat. What to do?

Ignore it? Never become attracted to a place, by its description?

To close in on the pure story all the time, and neglect its setting? This will be a hard decision, a difficult one. I don't know if it's possible.

The uninhabitable place of Anne-Marie Stretter, a Far Eastern scene, with a park of lepers, wrought-iron grates on the windows, a suite of drawing rooms, etc., it will never be found.

What is available to us is a sober palace that is Voltarian, French, temperate.

If we had a palace in Venice, the whole thing would be less difficult. We don't have one.

In short, I am faced with the impossibility of shooting *India Song.* This impossibility has always existed, of course. But now it becomes concrete: no *place* to shoot the film.

Therefore, a double impossibility: the intrinsic impossibility of the project itself; and then another impossibility—finding a concrete place to film it. The second impossibility is the corollary of the first.

The impossibility of finding a place to shoot, a place that can contain the film, verifies that content escapes all form, that it is a movement through all forms, forms of places, forms of actors. What to do?

Shoot at Pommereux?

Shoot at the Rothschild ruin in Boulogne?

If we shoot at Pommereux, the impossibility of finding the right place won't be glaringly evident. If we shoot in the Rothschild ruin this impossibility will stand out so much that it will seem like it was shot on a set.

Moreover, in the Rothschild ruin, the first impossibility (of penetrating the writing-about-Anne-Marie Stretter) will be *seen.*

The place has no verisimilitude, it is a place to flee from, it is uninhabitable.

At Pommereux the place will have the beginnings of verisimilitude.

People will say about Pommereux: this setting was a poor choice. They will say of the Rothschild ruin: they chose that setting to warn us of the nature of the story that will unfold there.

In the book, we stay in the empty set for a long time. Here, that won't be at all possible: at Pommereux the flatness and at Rothschild the intention will show through.

As I get back to the shooting script of *India Song* again, I am completely uncertain about the location of the shoot.

However, here it is. I am doing it according to the plan I've made: Pommereux.

NOTE II

The film *India Song* will be *built* with *sound* and then with light.

NOTE III

Whatever's happening must always hold the camera's attention outside the reception. It must *not* give the impression *of avoiding entering it* but of being interested above all in everything going on *outside* the reception. These events must be linked to one another continuously.

NOTE IV

The reception is a play of silhouettes made opaque by the mirror, as if whole bodies were moving, not just faces. The direction of the gaze, here, is the direction of the entire body.

REEL III (10 shots) 16'8″

Note: There are five kinds of *voices* at the reception. In the editing they were designated in this way:

A) *Privileged* voices, of bursting intensity; that is, those of the *conversations* between the people present (Anne-Marie Stretter, Vice-Consul, Young Attaché) or named (Ambassador, G. Crawn).

B) *Very clear* voices, that is, those that make a commentary—on the past—in the repeated shots (Viviane Forrester).

C) *Clear* voices—those of the guests—whose remarks are related to ongoing narrative.

D) *Muffled* voices—also of the guests—whose remarks have no direct relationship with the ongoing narrative: they speak of the heat, of India, but are in some way the "throwaways" of the C voices. These voices are often mixed with the murmur of the reception, and often only a few words surface.

E) Voices of *ambiance*—again, guests—that form what we call "blocs." These are general conversations, often concomitant with a given subject (heat, the beggar woman, European vacations, war, etc.). They were impossible to fragment, to divide, and only scraps of phrases come to the surface from them.

To simplify, the letter (A,B,C,D,E) that corresponds to each group of speeches will be put in the margin.

Empty Rothschild Esplanade
Night
"Tango-Tango"

C • The park extends to the Ganges . . . the offices are on this side . . . you see . . . these gray buildings . . . Farther off, the tennis courts . . . deserted during the monsoons . . .
• Almost no one dances.
• This heat . . . how do you expect? . . . the only remedy, immobility, slowness . . . slows the blood . . .

• This odor of mud . . . stale? . . .
• The Ganges . . . low tide . . .

Private sitting room
The Young Attaché and the
Young Guest arrive
Waltz "Wonderful Mary"

C • The new Austrian Attaché
  arrived a month ago . . . He
  isn't used to India.
• Is it the first time he's come?
• Yes. He'll be back, he'll go to
  the Islands . . .
• How can you tell? . . .
• That suffering in his eyes . . .
  She doesn't like people who get
  used to India.
• The Ambassador invites people
  to the Islands . . . for her, for
  his wife.
• She is going alone to the
  Islands. The Ambassador will
  go hunting in Nepal.
• They say her lovers are
  English, strangers to the
  Embassy circle.
• They say the Ambassador
  knows.

The Young Guest arrives

• A friend of the Stretters,
  unknown in Calcutta.
• The humidity is so . . . the
  pianos go out of tune
  overnight . . .
C • . . . The Vice-Consul of France
  in Lahore just entered the
  park. *(pause)*
D • . . . the heat, on awakening . . .
C • At the last minute she sent
  him a card: "Come."
• What did he do exactly?
• The worst . . . killing . . . over
  there, in Lahore.

33

D • As soon as one sees daylight,
nausea . . .
C • What is the official version?
• His nerves went. Often.
• Just that.
• What a face . . . as if grafted
on . . .
• He is very pale . . .
• She could have spared us his
presence . . .
• No one received him in
Lahore?
• No one.
• His removal was prevented just
in time . . . An intervention by
the Ambassador . . .
• India's closed circles always
make me think of leprosy.
• Perhaps he drank?
• No. Drunkenness is always the
same for everyone here, we all
talk about leaving . . . No, he
didn't drink.
• The Ambassador said to the
Young Attaché: ". . . I would
be pleased if you spoke to him
a little . . ."
• He would like to approach
him . . .
• He turns away . . .
• Can't bear it . . .
• No. Nothing.
• He laughs. Looks . . . as if he
were mad with happiness all of
a sudden. Perhaps he has just
seen Mme. Stretter.
• Now there's an idea . . .
• I just realized it now.

34

B • Has he talked about Lahore
with anyone?

• *(pause)* To her. At the end of
the night.

• At night he fired shots in the
Shalimar gardens, at the lepers,
at dogs. But bullets were also
found in the mirrors of his
residence in Lahore.

• He was shooting at himself (in
some way).

Private sitting room
Anne-Marie Stretter
enters

D • . . . in the early days, people
say the siesta is not worth the
trouble . . . and then . . .

B • Roses arrived every day from
Nepal. She distributed them at
the end of the ball.

D • . . . moreover, no one is
around at that hour . . . the
heat makes the head reel . . .
intoxicated.

• After lunch, one collapses . . .
this sleep . . .

• And yet everyone waits for
something like that . . .
India . . .

• . . . The storms, one waits for
them . . . just a hole in the sky
. . . that clogs up right
away . . . it begins again.

• . . . India is different the first
time, it's impossible . . . and
then . . .

C • How white the women of
Calcutta are . . .
For six months they only go
out in the evening, flee from
the sun . . . One would say she

was a prisoner of a kind of
suffering . . . No one knows
what happens behind these
walls . . . what she does . . .
(silence) bicycling very early
in the morning in the park . . .
tennis . . .
She reads, they say . . .
Packages of books addressed to
her arrive from Venice . . . She
is going to the Islands . . .
Appearances . . .

Tennis courts
"Rhumba of the Islands"

C • Only one person sees him. The
director of the European Club.
A drunkard.
 • Everything he said to the Club
Director was repeated to the
Ambassador.
 • It's odious.
 • You don't understand . . . He
spoke to the Club Director
because he knew what he said
would be repeated . . . A way
of reaching her, this
woman . . . He said he had the
same right to Mme. Stretter's
solicitude, to her love, as the
others, her lovers in
Calcutta . . . At night near the
tennis court . . . that bicycle—
he said: something she had
touched . . . no . . . that can't
be repeated . . .
She said nothing about this
passion . . . nothing.
 • He said he regretted not
explaining about Lahore in a
convincing way.

36

*Convincing?
* I remember that word
particularly.

Private sitting room
The Vice-Consul Enters
The Young Attaché Enters
They leave

C • What is known about his
background?
• Neuilly. His father was a small
banker. An only child.
The mother supposedly left the
father. Then she died . . .
Many expulsions from schools.
Reform school when he was
about fifteen. An aunt writes
sometimes . . .
C • Look, he's crying.
• One would think he doesn't
even know it.
• . . . that he is in a tearful
state . . .
A • *V. Consul:* What do you want
of me?
Young Attaché: To speak to
you.
V. Consul: About what?
C • His voice is toneless . . .
. . . as if he wanted to keep
himself from crying out . . .
A • *Young Ataché:* About your
impending nomination.
(silence, no answer)
V. Consul: You're not getting
used to it either?

Voice of the beggar woman,
then "India Song" played by
the orchestra, then night at
the Rothschild park.

Young Attaché: (troubled)
No.
(silence) . . . This heat, of
course . . . but also this
monotony . . . this light . . . no
color. *(no response, silence)*
Young Attaché: I had no

37

preconceived ideas when I left France . . . *(a long pause)*, but you . . . before Lahore . . . would you have preferred something else?

V. Consul: Nothing. Lahore is what I wanted. *(silence, no answer)*

Young Attaché: Come over to the bar. What are you afraid of? *(pause)* They say you would like Bombay.

V. Consul: I want to stay in Calcutta.

Young Attaché: I don't think that would be possible . . .

V. Consul: In that case I put myself in the hands of the consular authorities. Let them send me where they want.

Young Attaché: Bombay has fewer people, the climate is better, and it's much closer to the sea.

V. Consul: I have not asked about my dossier. What are people saying?

Young Attaché: They say that Lahore . . . what you did in Lahore, no matter how you look at it . . . no one . . .

Return to the private sitting room
Anne-Marie Stretter and Michael Richardson dance to "India Song" orchestra

V. Consul: No one? *(no answer, silence)*

Young Attaché: Come over to the bar. *(pause)* What are you afraid of? What are you doing? Come . . .

V. Consul: I am listening to "India Song."
I came to India because of this melody. That song makes me want to love. I have never loved. I had never loved.

C • He saw himself photographed in a rocking chair by the sea of Oman . . . And then one morning, going to the office, he saw her in the park, near the tennis courts, in white . . .

Chinese drawing room
Anne-Marie Stretter and
Michael Richardson,
embracing

C • What a story, what a love . . . they say he gave up everything to follow her . . .

D • Everything, in one night . . .
(Ambiance called: Touraine and Asturias)

E • . . . We're going to Touraine . . . between Amboise and Tours.

 • . . . It is very beautiful, I know it well . . . But for children . . . Britanny (is better).

 • . . . When one returns, what desolation . . . it's strange . . . France: a word . . .

 • It's true, next to what happens here . . . these gigantic dimensions that every event takes on . . . hunger, heat, sometimes passion as well . . .

 • . . . these suicides by Europeans that increase with the famines . . . from which they never suffer.

 • . . . somewhere inside oneself, this Western guilt . . . on an

individual level . . .
• . . . it's absurd, of course . . .

. . . .
• Shanghai . . . you saw? The
photographs of the last
bombardment?
• Yes . . .
B • The first attempt at
Savannakhet . . . because of a
dead child, abandoned by its
mother, a beggar woman from
the North, in the park of the
central Administration . . . in
front of her room . . .
E • . . . And the Japanese who
continue to advance. They are
at Pao Tchan.
• . . . What Goebbels said about
Bolshevism at Nuremburg,
some things are right, it's
undeniable . . .
• And about Spain too . . . In
fact, in Asturias
*(interrupted by the
Charleston).*

*Private sitting room
Vice-Consul and A.M.
Stretter
Charleston*

C • Death in the middle of life,
death that would never catch
up with us . . .
• What are you talking about?
• About the Vice-Consul of
France who is looking for
Madame Stretter.
• She often leaves receptions . . .
More and more, lately.
C • No woman in Lahore had
known him well enough . . .
could have said something . . .

· No one.
· How terrible it is.
· No one ever went to his
residence in Lahore. He
wanted it like that: a virgin,
alone.
Waiting to love.

End of reel III

REEL IV (10 SHOTS) 17′26″

*Empty set, then the Young
Guest enters, then he dances
with Anne-Marie Stretter
"Rhumba of the Islands"*

C · It had to happen . . . look . . .
The Vice-Consul is moving
toward Mme. Stretter . . . *(long
pause)*
· Did you see? What skill . . .
The Ambassador spared his
wife that thankless task.
· Where are they going?
· Into the second drawing room.
Notice that sooner or later the
Ambassador had to speak to
him . . . so . . .
· They are bringing them
champagne . . .
A · *Amb.:* If I have understood
correctly, my friend, you
would like to be sent to
Bombay? But, in Bombay you
cannot hold the same post you
did in Lahore; it's still too
soon . . . If you stay here . . . it
will be forgotten. If you want,
I'll keep you in Calcutta . . .
V. Consul: Yes.
(silence)
Amb.: You know, a career is

41

mysterious. (The more you want it the less successful you are.) If you forget Lahore, others will forget it . . .
V. Consul: (pause) I do not forget Lahore.
                    (silence)
Amb.: You're not getting used to India . . . *(no answer)* There are remedies for this nervous stress . . .
                    (silence)
In the beginning, everyone, myself included, is in the same position. One must find a way of looking at things . . .
V. Consul: I haven't found it. I see nothing.
                    (silence)
Amb.: Go back to Paris . . . It's easy.
V. Consul: No, it's impossible.
                    (silence)
B • The Mekong toward Savannakhet . . . It's a wide yellow stream between the forest and the rice paddies . . . At that time the launches went slowly . . . It took several days . . . As soon as dusk came, the mosquitoes . . . you couldn't see anything any more . . . clusters of mosquitoes stuck to the mosquito netting . . .
C • The Ambassador wrote . . . she is supposed to have discouraged him . . .
B • In the rainy season, the sky is so low you can no longer see

the river banks . . . the water is
muddy . . .
• When he met her she was so
young, and already he . . .
There was great affection
between them . . .
• He took her away from the
administrator at Savannakhet?
• *(pause)* We don't know much
about the story. Supposedly
she was in danger of dying at
Savannakhet . . .
• So young . . .
• Precisely . . .
A • *Amb.:* What do you say, we
should very much like to
invite you some time to the
Islands. Sometimes there are
newcomers we would like to
get to know better than
others . . . The residency dates
back from the days of the
Company . . . You must see it
. . . those islands in the delta as
well . . .
Young Attaché: I would be
happy to come.

Rothschild Facade

• Music is perhaps what she
would have pursued . . .
behind these walls . . . prisoner
of such an ancient
suffering . . . not painful . . . a
leper, of the heart . . .
• However, in the park
sometimes . . . those tears?
• The light of the monsoon . . .
so painful . . . and her eyes
were so pale . . .

43

Young Attaché and Anne-Marie Stretter enter. They dance. Frangie Waltz and then "India Song" orchestra

C • You can speak about her?
• Beyond reproach.
  Nothing in the open: that's
  what we mean by this word
  here.
• After Venice, she never gave
  another concert?
• No, never.
• Do they know each other?
• They must have seen each
  other in the park.
• What is he looking at?
  (English accent)
• The French Ambassador's wife
  who is dancing with the Young
  Attaché.
• If you listen closely, her voice
  has slight foreign inflections.
• Perhaps that's what makes her
  seem far away, her foreign
  origin . . .
• That too, yes, perhaps.
A • *A.M.S.:* I would like to be in
  your position, to be here for
  the first time, during the
  monsoon rains. *(pause)* You're
  not bored? What do you do?
  In the evening? On Sundays?
  Young Attaché: I read, I sleep
  . . . I really don't know . . .
  A.M.S.: (pause) You know,
  boredom is a personal thing,
  it's difficult to know quite
  what to suggest.
  Young Attaché: I don't think
  I'm bored.
  A.M.S.: And then . . . *(stop)*
  . . . perhaps it's not as hard as

44

people say. *(pause)*
Thank you for the packages of
books, you had them sent to
me from the bureau very
quickly.
Young Attaché: You're
welcome.
                    (silence)
A.M.S.: You know, almost
everything is impossible in
India . . . that's what people
say . . .
Young Attaché: What are you
talking about?
A.M.S.: Just . . . it's
nothing . . . About this general
despondency . . . It's neither
painful nor pleasant to live in
India . . . not easy or hard . . .
it's nothing . . . you see . . .
nothing . . .
Young Attaché: (pause)
You're saying it's impossible?
A.M.S.: Yes . . . perhaps . . .
but taken literally, that would
be an oversimplification . . .
                    (silence)
Young Attaché: The French
Vice-Consul in Lahore is
looking at you.
                    (no answer)
Young Attaché: He has been
looking at you from the
beginning of the evening.
                    (no answer)
Young Attaché: You didn't
notice him?
                    (indirect response)
A.M.S.: Where does he want to

be assigned? Do you know?

Young Attaché: Here in Calcutta.

A.M.S.: Really . . .

Young Attaché: I thought you knew . . .

> *(no answer)*
> *(silence, dance ends)*

Young Attaché: They say you are Venetian.

A.M.S.: My father was French. My mother was from Venice. I kept her name.

Young Attaché: I thought you were English at first.

A.M.S.: That happens sometimes.

> *(silence)*

Young Attaché: (pause) Are there people who never get used to it here?

A.M.S.: (pause) Almost everyone does.

> *(silence)*

My husband told you we would like to see you at the Islands.

Young Attaché: I would be very happy to come.

> *(silence)*

A.M.S.: You write, I believe?

Young Attaché: (pause) I thought I could. Before. *(pause)* Someone told you that?

A.M.S.: (pause) Yes, but I would have surely guessed . . . from the way you keep to yourself.

Young Attaché: I gave it up.
(pause)
Mr. Stretter used to write too?

A.M.S.: It happens that he did
sometimes, yes. *(pause)* And
then . . . *(stop)*

Young Attaché: (pause) And
you?

A.M.S.: (pause) I never tried.

Young Attaché: You think it
is not worth it, is that it?

A.M.S.: That is . . . Yes, you
might say so.

Young Attaché: You play the
piano?

A.M.S.: (pause) Sometimes.
(pause) Less so in these past
few years.

*Young Attaché: (an expert in
love already)* Why?

A.M.S.: It's difficult to
express.

(silence)

Young Attaché: Tell me . . .

A.M.S.: Music has had painful
associations for me . . . for
some time . . .

Photograph of A.M.S.

C • In Venice, still very young,
eighteen years old, music, you
know, to the point of madness
. . . leading to a kind of
suicide . . . still . . .

• She hasn't played for several
years, says she no longer knows
how.

• What is happening?

47

*Return to the shot of A.M.S.
and the Young Attaché
"India Song" orchestra*

• The Vice-Consul of Lahore
has invited the Spanish
Ambassador's wife to dance.

A • *Young Attaché:* They're
talking about leprosy. *(pause)*
Are you required to dance
with him.
A.M.S.: I don't have to do
anything . . . but . . .
Young Attaché: (pause)
Tonight he was in the park
near the tennis courts.
A.M.S.: (retreating) He sleeps
badly, I think.
Young Attaché: (pause) He's
still looking at you.
(silence)

C • She left him during the
dance . . .

• What happened?

• It must have been something
he said. Something that
frightened her.

• But what are people afraid of?

• It's not fear, really, it's
repulsion (it can't be analyzed).

A • *Young Attaché:* Is repulsion a
feeling you know nothing
about?
A.M.S.: (pause) I don't
understand . . . How can one
know nothing about it?
Young Attaché: The
horror . . .
Voice of G. Crawn: Come
over to the bar. I'm an old
friend of Anne-Marie Stretter.
Let me introduce myself: I'm

48

George Crawn. There's no one
at the bar . . .
C • He said that to divert him . . .
 • Look at him—ready to flee . . .
and at the same time . . .
Young Attaché: He's still
looking at you.
 • People say she doesn't dare go
into the park.
 • What are they talking about
with that man from their
club?
 • About childhood, and her . . .
the French Ambassador's wife.
 • What is he waiting for before
leaving the reception?
 • To be thrown out, it would
seem.

*(The beggar woman in the
distance, singing, rambling.)
Travelling shot. Night.
Hotel on the Islands
(Ambiance: the beggar
woman)*

E • A beggar woman entered the
park.
 • She's mad.
 • She's the one who laughs.
 • Look.
 • The sentinels are under orders
to let her enter.
 • Look.
 • She would have come from
Laos . . . which seems
impossible . . .
 • She's thin . . .
 • Very.
 • Her voice is youthful . . .
ageless.
A • *Young Attaché:* A beggar
woman entered the park.
E • . . . beggars in general, haven't
you noticed?

• Is she a leper?

• No, she doesn't seem to be one.

A • *A.M.S.:* I know . . . she's the one who sings, you know. It's true, you've just arrived in Calcutta . . . It seems to me she sings a song from Savannakhet . . . it's in Laos . . . She intrigues us. I tell myself that I must be mistaken, it's not possible . . . we are thousands of kilometers from Indochina . . . how could she have done it?

Young Attaché: (pause) I heard her in the street early in the morning . . . *(pause)* It's a cheerful song.

A.M.S.: The children sing it over there . . . *(pause)* . . . She must have come down through the river valleys. But how did she cross the Cardamones mountains?

Young Attaché: She is completely mad.

A.M.S.: Yes, but you see . . . she is alive. Sometimes she comes to the Islands. How? We don't know.

Young Attaché: She follows you, perhaps. Does she follow white people?

A.M.S.: That happens. For food.

(silence)

Ragtime. Michael
Richardson in Chinese
drawing room.
Alone.

• Where is he? (The Vice-
Consul)
• Near the bar. He drinks too
much, that man. It's going to
end badly.
B • We saw him at night through
our bedroom windows, walking
. . . at night as if in the middle
of the day . . .
• *(repeat)* . . . at night as if in
the middle of the day . . .
• He called down death on
Lahore . . . fire . . . he shouted
too . . . disconnected words . . .
he was laughing . . .

Private sitting room
The Vice-Consul enters and
looks at himself in the mirror

• Might there be, in everyone of
us, the chance, only a chance,
of being like him, when faced
with Lahore . . .
• Even so . . . one knows these
things, like leprosy, before
coming . . .
• No.
• Perhaps he didn't see that
there were people in that
garden . . . in that light . . . in
that kind of mist.

REEL V (7 SHOTS) 14′13″

A black pond

C • Look at the sky . . . sickness
. . . this density . . . this filth
. . . through the night.
• He told her he wanted to get
leprosy.

51

Private sitting room
A.M. Stretter and Michael
Richardson enter
They dance—Frangie Waltz

C • This man has fits of anger . . .
• About whom? About what?
• Do you think one always needs
  an object?
• Look . . . they're dancing.
• She has always liked to dance.
• Several months ago, at
  Chandernagor, they were
  found in a brothel . . .
  They wanted to die
  together . . .
• Seeing them, you wouldn't
  think so . . .
• Brought back in an ambulance
  to Calcutta. In the end,
  everyone knew . . .
• People said: for no reason, just
  an indifference to life . . .
• . . . or, the contrary . . .
• People confuse . . .
• No, there is a certain
  equivalence there.

Rothschild facade

B • She was talked about a great
  deal . . . this love . . . These
  Islands as well . . . these
  Islands in the Delta . . . their
  only regret when they left
  India . . .
  What would have become of
  them without them?
  The heat.
  The fear.
  The leprosy and the hunger.
  The Vice-Consul of Lahore.
  Those deaths . . .
  This sweetness . . . One
  wondered: her reading? her
  sleepless nights at the

("India Song" orchestra)

Black piano with "India Song" sheet music

Tennis courts. Night. Rain. Empty Set.

Private sitting room A. Marie Stretter enters Then, the Vice-Consul

residence in the Delta?
Those tears . . . ?
(pause)

"India Song" . . .
When he went to the office, he whistled "India Song" . . .

C • He said to the Club Director: at my house in Neuilly, in the drawing room, there is a black grand piano. "India Song" is on the music stand. My mother played "India Song." I used to listen to it from my room. The sheet music has been there since her death.

C • Look . . . Daylight already . . . no one is leaving . . .
 • It seems they are waiting . . .
A • _Voice 3:_ The tennis courts were deserted . . . A bicycle was there.
Voice 4: I noticed they were deserted after he passed by. There was a rending of the air. She looked at me.

A • _V. Consul:_ I didn't know you existed.
V. Consul: Calcutta has become a form of hope for me.
_A.M.S.:_ I love Michael Richardson, I am not free of this love.
V. Consul: I know. I love you like that, in your love for Michael Richardson._(pause)_
It doesn't matter to me.
V. Consul: I am speaking

53

falsely.
Do you hear my voice?
It frightens them.
A.M.S.: Yes.
V. Consul: To whom does it
belong?

(*silence*)

V. Consul: I shot myself in
Lahore, without dying from it.
Others separate me from
Lahore. I do not separate
myself from it. I am Lahore.
Do you understand too?
A.M.S.: Yes. (*pause*) Don't
shout.
V. Consul: Yes.
V. Consul: You were with me
before Lahore. I know it. You
are a part of me. And you will
shoot at the lepers of Shalimar
with me. What can you do
about it?
V. Consul: I didn't need to ask
you to dance to know you.
And you know it.
A.M.S.: I know.
V. Consul: It is completely
useless for us to go any
further. We have nothing to
say to each other. We are the
same.
A.M.S.: I believe what you just
said.
V. Consul: You have love
affairs with other people. We
don't need that.

(*silence*)

V. Consul: I wanted to know
the smell of your hair, which

54

explains why I . . .
(silence)
V. Consul: After the
reception, you stay on with
your close friends. I want to
stay with you once.
A.M.S.: That's not possible.
V. Consul: They would throw
me out.
A.M.S.: Yes. *(pause)* You are
someone they must forget.
V. Consul: Like Lahore.
A.M.S.: Yes.
V. Consul: What will become
of me?
A.M.S.: You will be assigned
somewhere far from Calcutta.
V. Consul: Is that what you
want?
A.M.S.: Yes.
V. Consul: Very well. *(pause)*
And when will it end?
A.M.S.: When you die, I
believe.
V. Consul: What is this
sickness? My malady?
A.M.S.: Knowledge.
V. Consul: Of you?
(no answer, silence)
V. Consul: I am going to cry
out. I am going to demand that
they let me stay here tonight.
A.M.S.: Do as you wish.
V. Consul: So that something
will have happened between
you and me. A public incident.
I don't know what to shout.
Let them know at least that
love can be cried out.

V. Consul: They will be
uneasy. *(pause)* And then,
they will begin to talk again.
V. Consul: I know you won't
tell anyone that you agreed.
(long silence)
V. Consul: Let me stay with
you!
V. Consul: I am staying with
her tonight, once, with her, do
you hear?
(shouts)
V. Consul: I'm staying at the
French Embassy! I'm going to
the Islands with her! I beg you.
I beg you, let me stay!
V. Consul: (howling) One
time! Just once! I have never
loved anyone but her. I beg
you . . . *(sobs of the Vice-
Consul)*
(shouts)
V. Consul: Anna-Maria
Guardi!
(slightly spaced out)
(over the shouting)

(Ambiance: the Vice-Consul's   E • What is happening?
cries)   • How terrible it is.
                                     • How offensive.
                                     • How awful, etc.
                                     (over sobs and
                                     cries)
                                     • Where is she?
                                     • In the private salon . . . with
                                     him . . .
                                     • They're taking him away.
                                     • He let himself be led away . . .
                                     • How strange it is . . .

56

* How indecent . . .
* Everything is clear all of a sudden.
* What is?
* Lahore.
* In a way, everyone should cry.
* But . . .
* It is a way of speaking . . .

Phrases spoken in English in a woman's voice

* Such a pain.
* Everything is her fault . . .
* No sense of . . .
* To court shame like that . . .

C • *Ambassador:* You ought to go home. I assure you, you have drunk too much.

REEL VI (6 SHOTS, 5 OF WHICH ARE WITHOUT TEXT) 15′29″

Chinese drawing room. Everyone, with the exception of the Vice-Consul. George Crawn's first appearance

Silence, then a lasting cry (to the end of the film).

Voice 3: Is it the Vice-Consul of France who's shouting?

Voice 4: Yes. Still.

Voice 4: We lose track of him after his trip to the Islands. *(pause)* He resigns from the consular corps. The dossier stops with his resignation.

Voice 3: (pause) Very quickly after . . .

Voice 4: A few days.

Cry (distant) Beethoven's 14th Variation on a Theme of Diabelli

Voice 3: What is he shouting?
Voice 4: Her Venetian name,
in deserted Calcutta. All night
in Calcutta, he cried out this
name.
Voice 3: The sound of
wings . . . of birds . . .
Voice 4: Daylight.
Voice 4: (very slow) The day
breaks here, around here.
(pause) And over there.
(pause) The air smells of river
mud. And leprosy. And fire.
Voice 3: Not a breath of wind.
Voice 4: No. The air moves
very slowly, circulating the
odors.
(pause)
Voice 4: The sun.
(pause)
Voice 3: What light. Terrible.
Voice 4: Yes, the light of exile.
(pause)
Voice 3: She is distracted.
Voice 4: Yes. Profoundly
absent.
Voice 3: The heat is the color
rust. Above, fumes.
Voice 3: This continent, hangs
suspended . . . ? below,
Bengal . . .
Voice 4: The monsoon.
Voice 3: Farther away. Lower.
Under the clouds . . . ?
look . . .
Voice 3: In a bend of the
Ganges, that white patch . . . ?
over there . . . ?
*Voice 4: (delayed)*The English

cemetery.

Voice 3: A car speeds straight ahead. *(pause)* Along the banks of the Ganges.

Voice 4: They left for the Islands.

(pause)
(silence)

Voice 3: Those junks?

Voice 4: Rice. *(pause)*

Voice 3: On the embankment, those dark spots . . .

Voice 4: People. *(pause)* The highest density in the world.

(silence)

Voice 3: The multitudes of dark mirrors . . . ?

Voice 4: Indian rice paddies.

(silence)

Voice 3: (pause) The black Lancia has stopped.

Voice 4: The rains. *(pause)* The roads are cut off. They took shelter in a Sala. It is there that the Young Attaché said, "I saw the Vice-Consul before leaving. He was still shouting in the streets. He asked me if I was going to the Islands. I said no, that I was going to Nepal with the Ambassador."

Voice 3: Did she approve of the Young Attaché's lie?

Voice 4: She said almost nothing about the man from Lahore.

(pause)

59

Voice 3: This patch of
green . . . It's getting larger . . .
Voice 4: The sea.
(pause)
Voice 4: The Islands. *(pause)*
It's the largest. The main
Island. They have arrived.
Voice 3: (pause) That big
white building . . . ?
Voice 4: The Prince of Wales
Hotel, the International
Palace. (The sea is rough.
There was a storm.)

RECEPTION: APRIL 1974 (SHOT 38)
POMMEREUX HOTEL (debut)

The camera is in the hall. Facing it, the entryway and, beyond, the park. Strong lighting. Total silence for several seconds, and immobility. Then, savagely, the uproar of the reception. Like an explosion.

Viennese Waltz

On the terrace, still far away, a dancing couple passes by, disappears. Then the couple passes by again. A servant with a tray crosses in front of the camera, coming from the reception (in the dining hall). Two couples drift into the reception, leave again. The camera does not move. Two women are on the terrace: they come down the stairs, turn, look at the reception. White fans. They disappear. The camera moves up to the edge of the terrace: it discloses the park where it again finds the women (the two above) who fan themselves. Two couples dance on the terrace. Some people in the back of the park. A servant passes with a tray of champagne goblets.

The camera pulls back and returns to the entryway slowly, it *thus defines* the perimeter of the reception, always at its left. The servant crosses in front of the camera in the opposite direction.

The women return, look in a certain direction, right camera, toward the private sitting room.

The camera keeps pulling back.

A young man, the Young Attaché, comes from the park. Alone. Stops. Looks in a certain direction, continues, stops, looks at the reception, then the park.

A man and a woman come out of the reception and look at the Young Attaché.

The Young Attaché goes into the reception. Disappears inside.

The couple follow him with their eyes.

The camera continues to pull back. It is in the hall, stops.

When it stops, the music (waltz) ends.

People come out, turn around, look at the place, curious.

The camera waits in the hall.

The corridors, the park and the hall empty out. The camera lets people come back toward the reception. Then, imperceptibly, it begins to advance.

Tango, loud.

In the entryway, alone, slowly, *the woman in black*, from the photograph, has arrived and looks at the private sitting room. She is coming from the park.[1]

Some seconds later, Anne-Marie Stretter, in white, arrives; she too looks at the private salon, then comes toward us, and smiles.

The two are on the set, the dead woman and the other. They did not see each other.

Anne-Marie Stretter: gesture indicating the heat.

Then she returns to the reception.

After her disappearance, the Young Attaché goes into the entryway, he comes from behind the camera, continues on, takes up a position facing the door of the reception and looks (Anne-Marie Stretter) (look of desire, of love). Anne-Marie Stretter had smiled at him.

The woman in black has gone into the private sitting room. No one is on the set. Tango, loud. The camera advances imperceptibly. Camera looks to the right: dark corridor.

Goes out, continues to advance.

Stops: in the distance, in the park, white silhouette of the Vice-Consul who moves forward.

He looks around.

All of a sudden the Vice-Consul stops (or) takes a step backwards; he has seen something.

Advance imperceptibly so we see what the Vice-Consul sees:

The Young Guest on the terrace and, farther away, two girls.

They look at him. Then avert their eyes.

---

[1]The photograph of this woman in black was supposed to be the dead woman's picture. I had asked Nickie de Saint-Phalle to play this role. The woman in black was seen at the reception. We saw her photograph only once in the first part. In the last shooting script, only the photograph remained.

Pull back slowly and Michael Richardson enters the shot. the private sitting room—very close to us. At this exact moment he recognizes the Vice-Consul.

The camera pulls back again. The camera then takes in the Vice-Consul, who looks hard at the reception. Both are in the shot: Michael Richardson and the Vice-Consul.

Tango, loud.

(Thus, Michael Richardson has been seen.)

Imperceptibly, at the same time that the camera advances, Michael Richardson goes toward the Vice-Consul. The Vice-Consul sees him from a distance. Michael Richardson stops on the spot. The Vice-Consul retreats. Michael Richardson pulls back, turns away. Sorrowful expression.

We lose sight of the Vice-Consul.

We wait and enter the dark private sitting room. Incense.

The woman in black is there. Cut to the woman in black.

Often cut to the woman in black during the reception.

With the end of tango,
the scene ends.

RECEPTION, JUNE 1974
(RUE CORTEMBERT)

(Beginning)

Empty set.

The Young Attaché enters the rectangle. Wanders alone in the empty space.

Looks at the place (as if preoccupied, a little lost).

Then looks in the mirror.

Then looks in the park.

Tango-Tango

The Young Attaché follows someone with his eyes. His gaze fixes on something.

The Young Guest comes into the rectangle.

Goes toward the piano near the Young Attaché. Also looks at the park.

A servant passes by and offers them some champagne.

They drink as they look at the park.

They have seen something. They look at a certain place in the park.

Take several steps (toward the park).

Stop.

Go out toward the park, as if they can't resist.

Empty set.

REPEAT SHOT OF 38

The grand facade of the Palais Rothschild, in ruins.

Murmurings.

"India Song"(orchestrated version) over the emptiness and the ruins.

The music fades.

Voices of the past.

SHOT 38 (cut in two during the editing)

Empty set.

Time passes over the emptiness.

Then, Anne-Marie Stretter arrives.

She positions herself so she is facing the central doorway.

Looks at the park.

She fans herself with a white fan.

Stops fanning herself. She has seen something too.

Fans herself again, looks at the park *in* the mirror.

Sees something again in the park. Stops.

Lowers her eyes, approaches the door.

Comes back, but always closer to us. Beside the mirror, always fanning herself, always in the position of being her own extra.

No longer looks at the park.

Stops near the photograph.

Moves off again.

Still looks at the park in the mirror. Stops fanning herself.

Lowers her eyes.

Leaves.

Empty set.

REPEAT OF 38 (reprise): Shot 20R Tennis Courts

Night

The tennis courts—pan—and farther away, Anne-Marie Stretter's red bicycle.

Rhumba

Voices of the guests.

Voices of the past.

Mixed.

SHOT 39

Empty set.

Then the Vice-Consul enters. Waits. Looks. Looks for her.

Crosses the rectangle.

Charleston

Reappears.

Moves toward the piano.

Looks at the photograph.

Goes toward the mirror. Raises his eyes. Looks up toward

the Chinese drawing room.

He appears to be crying, his eyes raised in a stare, with a terrifying expression.

This, for a long time.

Then he turns around. He lowers his eyes gradually.

She appears, at the other end of the rectangle. Very far away.

The Vice-Consul takes three steps. We see him from behind.

She stops. The Vice-Consul looks at her. Leaves.

He follows her with his eyes. Then, leaves in turn.

Empty set.

Translated by Edith Cohen

.

NOTES ON THE THEATER SET[1]
Marguerite Duras

It was supposed to be a place of forgetting and of faltering memory, that is, a place with uneven lighting, sharp beams of light with shadowy holes, breaks. Where things might happen that would not be announced.

A place, entered through intermediaries—the women and the voices—through their memory and their forgetting. They are shown the place, the scene, and they enter it. The theater is opened up to them; these voices enter and look. Recognize or don't recognize. They don't know us. And they speak.

Their role ends when day breaks. They evaporate with the light of day.

Others will enter and, in their turn, will look and speak, but without memory, without forgetting—the voices at the reception speak of a scene they alone see. These present voices, these voices of that space don't recognize us either. They tell us *what happens behind* the visible space, *around* us, *some yards* away, in this locked embassy in Calcutta in 1937.

As in the film, the theater will forgo extras.

India Song is a machine, it must function from the curtain's rising. But fully, immediately, without having to be geared up, without exposition. If we are not completely transported into the hole of *India Song*, we can never make up for delay.

The setting: a kind of loss.

Circles, intersecting circles.

The frustration even of the body of voices at the beginning, of the twin voices—this is *India Song*.

The chronology of the book seems to me best for the theater. Unless the sounds of the reception at the embassy are heard from the beginning.

The stage: it's empty. No one. Then, the singing of the beggar woman.

It's both empty and light. It's exterior and interior places at

---

[1]Written for Claude Regy

once; it's both fragmented and coherent. Doors. Closed. An enclosed place. One part of the set is like a forbidden city, as if the whole place were inaccessible. And it's true. Open doors. Smooth paths between the stones. Passages. An open piano; on the music stand is "India Song," half fallen off; from time to time, these accidents. A fallen object. A mirror shattered.

The decor is to be revealed little by little, fragment by fragment. A noisy accident should occur as it is revealed: a breaking pane that can't be seen breaking, far off. Or a silent visual accident: a dress slides to the ground and settles there.

The three cities of Peking—exterior, interior, forbidden. A divan displayed, ripped open, in plain daylight in the middle of Peking, the middle of the set. Dresses on the divan. Then perfumes. Incense. Then the beggar woman who sings while these places are revealed and who rambles on, far away. So that the two women, the two axes of *India Song*, merge into one. But like a dance at first, the "India Song" melody with orchestra.

Everything concrete. Nothing more concrete than death. A petrified set. Stopped in movement.

Pompeii.

What you lose in terms of space in the theater you make up for in disorder, you gain in various accumulations, in various noises. It is out of this jumble that *India Song* should emerge.

As if there were no set. Nothing calculated.

No linearity.

Through the mass, this excess, to work through this, through an *overflowing.*

NOTE FOR NOTHING
Marguerite Duras

How did I do it?

I don't know. All right, I don't know. I made it. Conscientiously, from day to day. This line, that piece of music, one had to enrich it, to hook voices on either side of it, define its boundaries. There were so many voices. I had to choose. Everyone talked about her, wanted her. Anna-Marie Guardi. And about him. I had to choose among the voices. It wasn't possible to represent or use them all. The reception was enormous at first. Then the numbers diminished. People spoke less. And when less was said, the park stood out more. Alleys were formed, dark, always dark toward the tennis courts and toward the gray buildings, the offices of the French Embassy. On the other side, the Ganges carried along the yellow earth of the rice paddies. Day and night. It was abominably hot in Paris in August. It was in August. I was preoccupied with questions of money. Hounded even as I worked. I have been making films without a salary since 1969. I *am* going to talk about this film. Don't be impatient, let me get rid of my annoyance, purify myself of wasted words. So I hated money, and the world. And the heat. And myself for being so stupid, for having always been that way, yes. Don't interrupt. I hated. This film that no one would see. No one sees my films. Why make them? Voices torment me. Another voice speaks to me when I wake up, saying, get out of here, get out of France, drop the whole thing. The voices waited to be heard. I no longer expected anything. At this point, I begin to come out of it, to see myself facing the film. I am doing it. Yes, facing the film. I am doing it. Each day, from morning until night. For three months.

Translated by Edith Cohen

DISPOSSESSED
An interview with Marguerite Duras
by Xavière Gautier

I want to ask you how you could do a film so different from others, how you could go so much farther than anyone else. I was surprised, you know.

Yes, but how shall I take that. Surprised, but not at all surprised, either. I have the feeling that it is four films at once, don't you?

It's strange, you know that, after reading the book, practically seeing you write it . . .

Yes, you were one of the first readers. Perhaps the second reader.

After reading it like that in a first draft, feeling very close to it, after seeing your other films, I was still very surprised. That is, it's well beyond what I could have anticipated, and you can't answer me there, that's why I say it's a stupid question because . . .

Yes, I can answer you. How did I proceed? By paying equal attention to each part and letting myself go, if you will, trusting in myself as much for a detail, in the finding of a detail, as for the overall organization.

Working yourself sick?

The hardest part was in September, after the editing. I spent a strange two weeks' vacation. It didn't go well at all. I was recovering, yes, recovering. The film was finished. It was big, it didn't need me any more.

Was it terrible?

Did I tell you what I dreamt? Once the film was mixed, that is, finished, audible, visible, I left on my vacation. Without showing it to anyone, I stayed away for two weeks. And when I came back, they screened the film a week later. The next day, for two successive nights, I had these dreams: the first night the place where I was living in Trouville, my little place, was burglarized. It didn't have windows any more, you couldn't see the sea, you had to climb up on a stool to see the sea; they even stole the property—it was much smaller—and all the furniture, the view. The next day, the second night, I dreamt that my identification papers, my money and my purse were stolen. I was on a train that was rushing along, no one cared about the theft. I was crying and people were saying to me, "See how she is, never happy."

That was just after showing it for the first time?

Yes, I had been dispossessed, not only of a given area, a place, my habitat, if you will, but even of my identity.

What seems strange to me is that you had these dreams when you were showing the film. Now, I had the impression, I don't know why, that it was when you were making it that you felt completely deprived of your identity, dispossessed.

Yes, but it wasn't public then. The fact that I had killed A. M. Stretter, that she was dead—others seized upon this when they saw the film. Until then I was the only one who knew that I had killed her.

Except that there was the book. So, you don't give of yourself in the same way in writing.

No doubt I don't. There was the stress of making the film, also the work, but I don't know, I proposed the hypothesis that it was Anne-Marie Stretter's death but. . . . Someone said this: It's as if she's been in mourning for three weeks, she killed A. M. S. But, as for the dreams of theft, it may be more than that, and a little different too. Perhaps they stole the identity of the person who wrote that, the person who, because of the film, didn't exist any more. The author of *Lol. V. Stein* and *India Song*.

It was funny because there was also the fact that they were stealing your light, so that you could no longer see.

Yes. While climbing on a stool, pulling myself up hard, I saw a sort of tide of solid cement, motionless, like an ocean of cold, dead cement. They were dreams of terror.

Of suffocation.

Yes, dreams that awakened me.

Nightmares . . .
How did it go in comparison with writing the book?

From the beginning of the film, the dialogue is the same as in the book. The voyage is the same, the death is the same. For the reception, I cut some of the dialogue, added other lines. For example, in the book there are gossips. There aren't any in the film.

I understand a little of what they are saying in the film, like different kinds of moving algae which surround A. M. S., you see water full of algae, tides. They don't touch her but it's as if she were in the middle, with everything swarming around her. It's completely oppressive. There's no ground for them to walk on. And then the guests seem attracted to her, touched. It seems to me that in the book it was more her social persona that made them talk.

In the book I spoke in general about leprosy and about suicides among Europeans, things like that, but all these very general conversations are part of what has been called the "lost conversations" in the film. We hear almost nothing of them. And then there are things that don't exist at all in the book. For example, you speak in the film of the Vice-Consul and you say, "He was near tears," and Benoît also says, "Everyone should cry."

The music, the voices, everything, the whole sound track is most extraordinary, I think, is most impressive. . . . The song of the Laotian, too. Another thing that's impressive is that one no longer recognizes known actors like Delphine. This is not Delphine Seyrig. You completely transformed her, as if she had gone through something that had killed her, that's it, and now she's another person, no longer herself, but a sort of phantom. Physically, she's scarcely recognizable. Of course, you recognize something about her, her elegance, her bearing, but at the same time, it's not she any more either. How did you direct her?

I talked to her. And I warned her right away that she wasn't Anne-Marie Stretter, that she represented something which approached her, but she wasn't playing the role of this woman be-

72

cause it couldn't be played and that that photograph of her was perhaps the real A.M.S. They all understood that they all had to be completely attentive. All of them. Automatically, when they entered the arena. The scene was prepared by a flood of words because I explained each time on the tape recorder what we were going to do. Then there was the music. Now, when they entered, they were really charged with presence, with meaning, weight. But the film must still elude me a little bit, it's true . . . the film itself. I was a little bit astonished by the kind of unanimity about it. I was surprised. I didn't think you would like it so much.

You know I went mad thinking it would stop. I wanted it to go on forever.

Dionys says I was completely lucid when I made it, that it's a very lucid film and completely willed, determined. That this is striking.

And what do you think?

I don't think that's ever true.

It's strange, you're also very precise. As you said, you wanted to carry out each little detail; and you did, it's very, very precise, meticulous; and at the same time, so you say, you were astonished that when you saw the whole thing, there was something bigger than that.

For instance, a precise detail: When she dances the rhumba with the Young Guest and she smiles, I recalled death, Savannakhet. That is, I thought back to the Mekong between the rice paddies and the forest, a large yellow stream, etc. You see, this is what working over a detail is. I said to myself, I'm going to put that in, it will be the theme of death, the deadly pivotal point which returns, which cries out still. And I did that with a great deal of care. It's obviously frenzied. She dances the rhumba, they talk about the Mekong at Savannakhet, and the muddy water. But, here I was, busy, you see, putting in my sentence, concentrating on the work that was needed, just putting it between the two words and a third sentence that meets the first and lets it fall on its feet as the fourth comes along. It was hard, you know. Well, I didn't realize the audacity it took to talk about the Mekong in the middle of a rhumba.

73

All the more impressive because a rhumba is supposed to be ridiculous.

Like a rhumba on a tennis court.

The images are superb, superb, superb, more beautiful than in all your other films. It seems to me that there is even more work involved in this one.

Yes, yes, I had much more time to prepare it.

It's perfect.

Usually I have a month. This time I had four.

What's curious is that it has a richness that is lacking in the others. Also, it's a little different from what you usually do. For example, all the dresses with the jewels. Already in La femme du Gange, *there was the overturned table and the veils . . . this was surprising considering the film as a whole, but here there are richer images, like the dresses, the houses, the objects. . . .*

The variety of places; I had more money.

Yes.

I shot in four different locations. That's real money: twenty-five million, the cost of a short film. And then it's true that I wanted to create not only a story as in *La femme du Gange,* the story of a person, a thing, an event, a love, and the traces it left behind. I wanted to do something more. I wanted to create the Vice-Consul of France in his secret relationship, in his closeness to A.M.S., the heat, the leprosy, India. You see, I wanted to do everything. I used a great deal of music and then the words would come and build. It was a great joy to make.

You achieved something truly extraordinary in that not one of the characters opens his mouth to speak; I'd like to know why it's so striking, why it's so impressive—the fact of seeing all the people in front of you, not one of them speaking, while you are hearing the voices.

But when Anne-Marie Stretter dances with the Young Attaché, you didn't immediately understand that they weren't speaking.

But I did.

When it is blown up to 35mm, it will be easier to see. Because in 16mm, they are rather far away.

In any case, you recognize the voice of Delphine right away.

But they were listening there.

They're listening to their own voices.

Ah yes, while they acted they listened to their own voices.

It must have something to do with death. Their voices are like ghosts. The voice is ghostly.

Yes, But I don't know if it doesn't also have something to do with cinema. There is something in silent films that has been lost forever. There's something vulgar, trivial in the phenomenon of sound.

In the realism.

Yes, the inevitable realism of sound . . . and the trickery it represents. So you see, when they speak and they hear their own speech, the speech resonates infinitely more. That is, at the same time they are supposed to be saying one thing, they might be saying something else. The scope is enlarged, the scope of speech is infinitely enlarged. I think that's what it is, and from this fact everything takes on a double meaning.

In the end, it's like the image. The very great number of images that are filmed in the mirror.

Yes.

It's somewhat the same thing, it opens the image.

The mirror is the axis of the film.

They are there, with a very strong presence, yet it's never they.

That's it. It's as if there is a constant shifting. If you take, for example, a very close shot of the Vice-Consul who weeps when he waits for her to come down the stairs, you feel there that it's a real sound, without which the film would lose something, and here I find it strengthens it. There's a shot, my favorite shot—it's at the end of the night when she's lying against the piano, exhausted— where she appears at the side of the image on the left side of the shot, very close up, and suddenly she's swallowed up and the second she disappears she's in the mirror, very far off.

You know, one feels utterly lost.

I thought I couldn't experiment further with a mirror. But, yes, I could take it that far. I didn't do it for effect. It just happened. I never changed my sets because of the mirror, things passed through it or they didn't, but the mirror was there.

You know I felt very lost in these places. You can't even ask yourself if she's in the mirror or on the other side. You let the character come, he becomes double. Suddenly he is very close, indeed. It has a curious effect on the body itself, you know, a little like vertigo or like being thrown out of joint when you miss a step . . . parts of the body, you see, were displaced.

A sudden jump. Yes, the difference between Seyrig and the photograph on the one hand, and that between Seyrig and A. M. S., is a little bit like the difference between sound and its reverberation; it's the same displacement, this reflection.

But how did you do the editing? That is the most mysterious part of the filmmaker's work to me. What do you do when you have the images? How do you cut?

That's all editing is.

It seems to me that I would never want to cut anything.

Oh yes, if you count five or six seconds, she has just gone out; six seconds she has to come back, you make her come back. Ten seconds, it's already too late; we have already forgotten the V. C. He must be there, present in the mirror. He returns. So their paths must have crossed outside. You see, it's a sort of constant balancing or equilibrium.

The film is very balanced. It is perfectly honest; no one

escapes.

It's because of the diversity of meanings, I think, the distribution of meaning. You have three meanings which come at the same time, three sentences spoken by the guests or commentators, the informants, and you, the spectator, must integrate them. The tennis court, for example: there you're told he touches the bicycle, and right afterwards, about his education in Neuilly. You must do your job, you must follow along. I don't know whether the spectator has to be very sophisticated to see it.

You're right inside something. Everything is there, the death of A. M. S., the death of India, death in India, the cry of the Vice-Consul. You see, the Vice-Consul's cry, how can it not cut through everyone? It explodes, breaks everyone open. It cuts through all the actors and the audience. We think it will never be over, never finished. All this part is extraordinary, until the kiss, the voyage, the end of the night, I'd say. You know, when they find each other later, when she is stretched out on the sofa in the little room upstairs and there are four or five men in black around her, standing still, I think it makes you afraid to be a woman there.

Almost interchangeable, the men.

Yes, all in black.

Or else, all in white.

Where is woman in this film?

In the one who dies.

It is she, in any case, who makes everything happen, makes the men move. At the same time . . . she disappears in the whirlwind she provokes.

She withdraws from it, rather, leaves it behind. She calls attention to the common malaise; I'm talking about the sickness that she and the Vice-Consul share: knowledge. "Of you?" he asks. She doesn't answer. In my opinion, "to understand her" is to understand everything. She is everything, the place, the moving place of my writing itself, that is, inexhaustible . . . I had to kill to stop it. I'd tried that in *L. V. S.* but I didn't succeed. There I'd really understood as I worked that it was the very foundation of my writing, writing about her.

Does that mean that you can no longer write any more about A. M. S.?

She can be written about now, but differently. She can always be written about, but not by me.

Do you know why you did that?

I don't even know what my relation to her is. L.V.S. was the most important, for you, for Michele, and for a lot of people, but she remains a child, doesn't she?

Yes, yes, absolutely.

And isn't A. M. S. completely mature? I don't know where the fascination she exercises comes from; it's up to you people to say.

You could know for yourself. It's difficult. Why she fascinated you at first, why you brought her forth from yourself.

But didn't I say in *Les parleuses* that I had known A. M. S.? I was in Vinhlong and one day the general administrator changed. He arrived with his wife. Their names were Stretter, perhaps. I don't know any more. They had two daughters. She was an extremely pale, red-headed woman who didn't wear makeup, who didn't try to attract attention. The being and appearance, if you will, I saw it there, I felt it there. Shortly after their arrival at Vinhlong I learned that a young man had just committed suicide for the love of her. This invisible woman, you see, who wasn't noticed and who attracted me because of the lack of color in her face, in her eyes, well! I understood that she had a power like the power of death, very much hidden, concealed, and I remember what an extraordinary shock the suicide of this young man was. So you see this woman, the French Embassy, the general administration of Vinhlong, the Mekong, the Ganges, and also the tennis courts in the park of the general administration. My brother played tennis there because he played well. I never went there, the teachers' children didn't go there, you had to be the child of a lawyer or doctor to enter the general administration.

And did your brother go there?

Yes. My brother was handsome and he played tennis well. So an exception was made for him. It was this woman who led me to penetrate the double meaning of things. From every point of view. She led me to writing, perhaps. Perhaps it was that woman.

Whom you saw for an hour!

I saw her in the streets, going from the post to the back of her limousine with her chauffeur. Oh, I was a microbe, I was seven years old.

And you were seven years old.

Wait, it was perhaps a little later, I may have been as much as eleven. I can't tell you; I can't remember very well.

But you were a little girl!

In any case it was like the primal scene that Freud speaks of. The day I learned about the young man's death was perhaps my primal scene. You know, she was a sensible, reasonable mother, and these two little girls, always in white, were her children; and this man, her husband, was a father. (I had no father and my mother lived like a nun.) She was the mother of little girls who were my age, and she had a body with the power to bestow death.

There were receptions, all in the regular order of things, the tennis courts, the park, the Mekong, the outings, the tour of inspection every evening, the European Club, so sad, along the Mekong . . . Everything was regulated, ruled like a sheet of music. All of a sudden, in a kind of perfect and, for me, how can I describe it, fixed universe, the accident: a suicide for the love of this woman. A young man kills himself for her. Everything was immediately covered up, there was a rumor that ran through the post. Then no one spoke about it any more. I didn't look in the directory to see if there were any Stretters.

But you think it could be a memory, not an illusion?

No, I am sure. Her name could perhaps be Stretter and that wouldn't surprise me. She must have been a woman from the North, with a complexion so light, no freckles, pale. For it to have

79

been such a shock, you see, I tell myself that it must have affected me for it to have reappeared forty, fifty years later, it must have affected me very, very deeply.

Why did the double meaning strike you like that?

With the very established, very visible colonial ostentation that surrounded me, this power of woman was not apparent; it was unexpected, it exploded just like that, like a bomb, but silently, you see. This accident wasn't ascribable to anything, nor could it be classified; it was natural, it had the fantastic violence of nature. It was either the cars of the rich or the cars of the poor, the children of the rich or the children of the poor, everything was like that, classified, codified, very clearly. And all of a sudden there was this accident within this order which had nothing to do with the kind of arrangement of white social life in the posts. I think this is what struck me. It overwhelmed me. It's strange, I have the impression that if her daughters are dead, I am the only one to remember it. Sometimes I ask myself, how can I verify it? I know that it happened.

But the young man didn't kill himself in that post; he killed himself in a post farther to the north where she had been stationed with her husband.

The story followed her?

We knew the story afterwards, we heard about it in Vinhlong. She gave the impression that she didn't belong in colonial society. Gave the impression that she read. In my books, all the women who read come from her. She went out alone, she had no friends; she entertained, there were official receptions. She had lovers but she had no woman friends, you see.

But you don't think that up to a certain point she resembled you? I don't know if you want to talk about it. You told me, the first time A. M. S. appears at S. Thala, she dances, dances; she sees nothing. You actually told me that you danced like that with a man, you couldn't see anything around you.

I don't want to talk about that.

This woman in white in her limousine, I see everything again; it's rather beautiful. The Club, too, with the enormous terrace on the Mekong. The deserted straight paths planted with ta-marinds, the white quarter.

I see Delphine there as you tell me about it.

There are moments when she is astonishingly beautiful. When she sees the Vice-Consul come toward her . . .

And it's strange to see her when they are lying down and her breast is naked. . . . He touches her, she goes back to sleep. How violent it is, violent. . . . It's unbearable.

Did you see the little necklace she wore? The heart beats inside. With each beat of her heart, the necklace jumps, glitters. There were two shots of the breast: one very abstract, filtered; and then the one that was edited. She must have nursed her child, there is a little slump on the end of the breast, a sort of bruise and one sees the sweat, the shot too filtered.

How were you able to leave this film?

I don't know if I have left it. I'm completely dazed, I sleep badly. I have nothing to do. Oh! I am going to make another film, but I don't think I will ever make one as beautiful. It's a little distressing. Do you think it will have as much of an impact as *Hiroshima?* Perhaps . . .

From what point of view?

As an event.

Oh yes! more. It's true that, at the time, Hiroshima *was the event; yes, at least like* Hiroshima.

You think so?

Oh yes! You know you can't see other films after it. It becomes completely stupid to see other films afterwards.

That's what I'm told.

You know, they're so far behind, terribly banal.

It makes me ill to see films . . . because of all the trouble they may have taken.

Next to yours, any other film lacks impact. You know, I had

81

trouble seeing anything again after India Song.

I don't go to the cinema anymore. I watch things on television.

You know, I see India Song's *images constantly as I speak. I see the images when she's in the hotel after, in broad white daylight, everything becomes white, her face when she looks out the window.... We see her in close-up, her face, and there is talk of Italy, of Venice ... of the light ...*

... As she walks in the corridor, too ...

Yes, the images of a fan, as well as when she is in her peignoir, barefoot.

When I shoot, I have no reference point. I think it comes from what I'm doing, it comes from that.

No reference to what?

To other things. I was saying to Viviane Forrester that naturally I have confidence in myself as I have confidence in others or in nature. You see, I have confidence in nature, I move toward it, I am part of it like everyone, so. . . . Why not also have confidence in myself?

You take the plunge.

Yes, but I risk nothing. I have nothing to save. Not my reputation. I don't care about it. Nor money, there isn't any. So I do what pleases me. People never do what pleases them.

It's true, that is one of the things that is most persuasive about you. More than persuasive. You are a woman who lives according to her desires and that's very rare. You want something and live accordingly.

Yes, yes, just like now, I've been cloistered for weeks. I live like that. Yes, really, it's rare when I force myself.

It's uncommon for people to live like you do.

I get the jitters about not having any money. But when I shoot, all that's swept away. Then, because I am radically incapable of making a commercial film, I can't imagine how they do it. . . . Some filmmakers are half in their films, or else in a panic because of references to such and such a cinema, director, story, era, audience. They even know which audience they are writing for, they don't forget which distributor they're going to have, etc., for fear that they might disappoint. It's not possible to work like that, because they want to make a profession of it, you see? But now I'm going through a crisis nonetheless, because I say to myself: here's one more time no one will be able to understand my film, rather, to see it; once again it will stay in the cine-clubs. But the film is finished, so it isn't a serious problem. And maybe not, maybe this time . . . there are distributors who want it already.

I can't imagine anything commercial, but I can see something with a larger audience, a sort of revelation. I was saying that you were very avant-garde, not only from the point of view of film, but to have made something which is at the same time text, film and theater. And it's not going to be at all easy to do the play after the film.

I am in the cinema up to my neck, and I no longer think in terms of the theatrical stage.

Whereas you saw it when you wrote it.

That's why I never plan anything in advance, and it's planned. Yes, I want everything, but I don't want this orchestral dimension of *India Song*, I never wanted it that way. You see, I generally never plan in advance. I never know where I'm going, and then, it's finished. All the same, it's strange how there is a savoir-faire which is in me, yet escapes me. That is, I must know where I'm going, somewhere inside me I know where I'm going. You see, when I say I don't know where I'm going, that's not right. I don't know how I'm getting there, but I know where I'm going, that's it. Ah! yes, from the first line of *India Song* I knew where I was going.

You see all that?

First, I see the theater, well, I saw *India Song* as theater, and then I wrote the book. Afterwards, the vision of the theater was replaced by a vision of the pages—recto-verso, recto-verso of the writing itself. And then, when I made the film, all that was swept away. Only the places in the film remained, very precise places, left camera, right camera, medium shot.

This film has something more than the other films you made. So why do you think it can cancel out La femme du Gange?

Someone told me that it was not going to cancel out, "to destroy" any of the others, except *La femme du Gange*, yes.

What do you think?

I haven't thought about it. It appeared nevertheless to be the beginning of something real, the utilization perhaps of a plurality of voices, the voices orchestrated on several levels.

But why does it cancel out the other one . . . because ever since L. V. S., *the same story begins again and again.* The Vice-Consul *never cancelled out* L. V. S. *and* L'amour *never cancelled out* The Vice-Consul.

But *La femme du Gange* is *L. V. S.*

Yes, India Song *doesn't cancel out* The Vice-Consul.

I wonder.

Oh, not at all!

I like that better because you realize what kind of a frightful career I would have if each time I did something it killed the preceding thing.

Or else you have to consider writing like Caroline chérie *where there is a sequel and it is supposed to be about something else . . .*

We were talking about the annoyances, the criticisms, the things that make you angry and which are obviously out of proportion. For me, it's the gap between theoretical and practical knowledge. I gave you as an example the story of a guy who does a luminous dissertation on nineteenth-century German philosophy and who afterwards opens up a can of sardines upside down. Well, that can of sardines would completely blow away the German philosophy. And really, I'll never get over that. And you said it's as if he deceived you. I think it's very true. It's strange how I can never forget the can of sardines. So, I'll tell myself with reservations maybe he is very brilliant, yes, but . . . It's strange, these accidents one can do nothing about.

Maybe I think this way because when several people who tried to recite the texts and who apparently understood them opened their mouths to read, I saw that nothing was understood, so I began by giving a tone, the way you indicate a musical key, you know, the *la*. And they didn't hear. My behavior with them completely changed. On the other hand, people with whom I had distant relations, I mean not at all continuous ones, and who read the text, immediately read with the right voice, with the desired simplicity; well, nothing can shake the esteem I had for these people.

It must be important to train the voices, something quite different from training actors.

An enormous difference.

Was it easy?

I didn't choose actors for the voices because actors act. I didn't want any of that. I had to get that out of the way. Yes, it's difficult, you keep ten sentences. You begin again. You say it very, very well right from the start.

In a film there are a lot of manipulations, a lot of physical actions, a lot of movement. You always run into this, a fool, some idiot who doesn't know how to walk and gets caught in the cables and that rules him out. You can't stand him; he breaks a machine, or worse, the machinery; or he says something the wrong way. But, there I was, helped by my actors; when Matthew enters, ah well, he really enters. He's there. And he fills the space. He said one thing very well. He said to us: "She told us to cross, cross the space. We began to go across and suddenly it felt like there was a cigarette pressed between our lips, that we had hands, arms, legs, and we had to make them work at the same time. And everything became important, the cigarette pressed between the lips." I never told them: "Cross," just like that. I said to them, "Daylight is coming, you are very tired, the Vice-Consul is crying out in the streets of Calcutta. You are going home. You stop a minute. You listen to the noise. He's still shouting very far away. You cross, you simply pass by."

When I think of Matthew, I always see him poised on the edge of the image like a bird. When I see Didier, he's looking at her, as if his vision were suddenly blocked. He wants to see behind her smile and he sees death. These are the anecdotes.

These entrances and exits are continual.

Yes, constant, they never stay where they are.

They never stay put. What they do most is to dance. They pass by as they dance or they walk by.

They look a lot.

They look, they listen.

Ah! they look at the park a lot. There are people for you in the park, now?

Yes.

But were you present at the shoot?

I came only one day. It was the first scene. It was when Delphine dances with Claude Mann, and Didier Flamand is there, against the mirror, watching them. It was very, very beautiful. I arrived at eleven o'clock in the morning, I left at seven. And that's all that was shot. I said to myself, how is she going to do it? She shoots her films in eleven days . . .

I spent two weeks in all; to date, it's my longest shoot.

Two weeks for this production!

Oh! you'll surely make a film sometime.

That would surprise me. I think it would be so strange to make a film. How do you do it?

You need complete confidence in yourself, you must have confidence in yourself. It's within everyone's reach.

Why doesn't everyone do it then?

Because their desire is not strong enough to let them forget their fears. For me it's strong enough. That's the whole difference.

Translated by Edith Cohen

SON NOM DE VENISE
DANS CALCUTTA DÉSERT
(Her Venetian Name in Deserted Calcutta)
Marguerite Duras

It began after *India Song*, with the impossibility of filming again, or writing. I didn't know what was happening to me. I no longer wanted to make films or write.

It was after having discovered this constraint, after having suffered and submitted to it, long after, months later, that I discovered it had something to do with *India Song*.

I still don't understand clearly what happened to me. But I discovered this: there was something I had to continue in *India Song*. I'd begun something with that film that I hadn't finished. I had landed somewhere but hadn't continued to advance. I had begun to make a breach in something but I hadn't dug deep enough, etc. I lived with these questions, this difficulty, for many months; then, it seemed to me that what was attempted in *India Song* was the reverse side of narrative, and this wasn't accomplished. I told myself that I had found the reason for my difficulties but I didn't say, after all, that I had to film this new *India Song*.

This possibility, this prospect of a new *India Song*, frightened me, I must say, and when Pierre and François Barat, to whom I spoke, proposed that I film it, film the story that I'd told them, and that they would produce it, I believed that producers could be as mad as directors. I was suspicious, I hesitated for two or three months. I was afraid, and told myself I didn't have the right to let them embark on an adventure like that. They insisted, and in the end I filmed *Son nom de Venise dans Calcutta désert*.

The places I showed in *India Song* were on the verge of ruin, they were unconvincing, people said they weren't habitable. But in fact if one looked closely at them, they were not so unhabitable and, if need be, one could live there. In *Son nom de Venise* these places are definitely uninhabitable. The swallowing up by death of places and people is filmed in *Son nom de Venise dans Calcutta désert*.

In other words, I filmed the desertedness of places in *Son nom de Venise*. All the same, you could assume that Anne-Marie Stretter lived there, you could imagine that she lived in these places that are now completely destroyed, that she might have been seen at a time when windows opened and let in light, when openings were practicable.

In the first *India Song*, death runs parallel to the film, you see it from time to time, but it isn't filmed head on. There are roses, photographs, incense, but not holes or abysses, no pile of broken windows, dust, chinks in the walls, spiders' webs. And the people there are assumed to be who they might have been, and they bear the names spoken in the film: the name of Anne-Marie Stretter, or of Michael Richardson.

The vertigo that comes with making a film like *Son nom de Venise* makes it difficult to return to staging actors in a set narrative, a classical narrative. While I was making the film I thought, I'm getting nowhere. I'll end up nowhere. There are people mad enough to produce me. But I'm going toward a sort of No Man's Land of cinema where there will no longer be any correlation between sound and image, toward a kind of dislocated cinematic time. I admit that when I saw the first reel edited I was in a deeply emotional state. I no longer understood anything, neither what I had done nor what the others were doing.

I see *Son nom de Venise* as if it were someone else's film.

There will be, with this film, a cleavage between those who support it, those who see it, who can see it, and those who can't. It began with *India Song*, and my sense of uneasiness came from the fact that it wasn't finished. Now that I've completed what I began, I see that *India Song* was half way to something I always wanted. The second picture cannot detract from the first. It's different. It's a different place. It's a different echo chamber. I think that in general there is a false relationship in film between image and sound, I am completely persuaded of that. Image and sound are in an unconvincing relationship in the films I see. Moreover, we always separate them when we speak about a film. People say the image is beautiful, but the sound isn't good; the scenario is not convincing while the image is beautiful. I don't understand at all what this means. It's as if they said, the typography of this book is beautiful but the content isn't good.

If you really want to hear *India Song*, hear the range, the exact amplitude of it, it's *Son nom de Venise dans Calcutta désert* that expresses it. I have the feeling I'm hearing the script for the first time and people say, what's happening, you changed the sound, we hear it better but it's absolutely the same. What there is to *see* in *Son nom de Venise* doesn't obstruct the sound. In *India Song* or in *La femme du Gange*, there is something in the image that keeps the sound from going as far as it could and fully taking its place. Here that ends, the sound wholly prevails.

I was completely haunted by the chateau; it was becoming an obsession. Things are going better now because *Son nom de Venise* is finished and I've since launched another film. My obsession with that chateau lasted a year; I went back to it with other people several times. It was a place of inexhaustible images.

When I made *Son nom de Venise*, it was perhaps not that something was happening to me, but that something was happening in film: I had the feeling that I was entrusted with it, charged to accomplish a destruction, the meaning of which had escaped me.

The conditions were very hard, it was $-7°$ in the ruined chateau when we filmed it and we didn't know where we were going, but the unanimity was fantastic and everyone went ahead, did the filming, and we finished it.

I spoke to people around me about my project, this second *India Song*. There were some who asked, why make another *India Song*, and others who were irremediably enthusiastic about the project.

It's true, there is such understanding between Bruno Nuytten and myself that without him and Joël Quentin, his assistant, I would undoubtedly never have made this film. The evening of the first rushes he said to me, "I unlearned five years of film school today." I have the feeling that *Son nom de Venise* was shot outside cinema, that Bruno and I went elsewhere to look for a kind of lost freshness, a clean breeze, and we brought all that back to cinema.

The film is seen and heard by women. The women you see in the last five minutes of *Son nom de Venise dans Calcutta désert* have come to see the film; they are in a state of impassivity, they are passive, thus completely integrated into the story and don't pass judgment on it. They watch, they listen, *they were there, we did not know it*. That's how I experience it, as "yes, they were

89

there." From the beginning of time, they listened and looked, they were there and will still be there after the film. They came to see their colleague, our sister Anne-Marie Stretter, die. They are going to look, look at her; in a shared understanding they are going to see her die.

What the images here have in common is that they are always a space offered but never occupied, the panes of glass present something like a passageway, but no one passes through. The shots of large white spaces, the drawing rooms show floors on which no one dances, no one lives, but where things are said. The mirrors are huge spaces into which no one looks. The esplanade is a big uncovered space where no one goes. If there is a unity in the image, it is that.

I thought it was simple, that everything coming from the image could illustrate, serve as a support for, the sound in *India Song*. No. The only thing in the film that's *full* and not *hollow* is the statue, and actually that's what we had the most trouble positioning. So we put it on the river, the Mekong, with the mosquitoes, the launches, that is, on the Savannakhet set, the Mekong, down which Anne-Marie Stretter had come at the beginning of her life.

Carlos d'Alessio's music attains a different dimension here; it's treated like raw material, like words: everything takes place as if the words and the music, like the places, were there a long time before the film began. In the film there's an equal respect for places and for sounds.

I remember when we filmed the first stage, there was a piece of cloth that hung awkwardly from the wall. I went over to the image and put the cloth back in a vertical position, and everyone cried out because it was part of the set. I never touched anything after that. If a branch got in the way, we all moved over to film another one. We never touched anything, whatever it was. We truly glided through it, encoiled in time, changed nothing, modified nothing, and so things came to us more easily. We didn't cheat once. Everything you see in the film is still there and everyone can go there to see it and recapture what we did; it's all there, intact.

The first thing that Geneviève Dufour and I did during the editing was to *name* the film's principal reference points. The lateral traveling shot across the chateau immediately became the "vessel" and then the "*body*" of Anne-Marie Stretter. The traveling shot across the lower part of the facade became the *cries* of the Vice-Consul. The gold and white ceilings, the *Venice shot*. The shot of the chinks in the walls became the *shot of the whiteness of Calcutta's women*. Next, the other shots began to whirl around the principal reference points—those of the park, the windows, the balustrades, the debris, the trees, the holes, the spider webs, the broken windows, the corridors. We continued to name the close-ups: Necropolis, Egyptian Shot, Great White Shot, Schwartz's, Braque Window, Violet Window, Cedar of the Vice-Consul, Leafy Park, Charming Pavillion, Large Panel Sky of the Voyage.

We grew up, became adult, along with the film. At the beginning we were both like children facing the whole mass of materials, and then we learned to see them, use them, speak with them. After several edited versions, we kept this one which will be: *Son nom de Venise dans Calcutta désert*.

Compiled from conversations with Marguerite Duras by Pierre and François Barat.

Translated by Edith Cohen

MOTHERS
Marguerite Duras

Difficult to talk about one's own work. What to say? I will speak of her, of the mother. The mother in *Whole Days in the Trees*, and the one in *The Sea Wall*, is the same. Ours. Yours. Mine, as well. The one I knew and loved was French. She was a woman from the north of France. A daughter of Flemish farmers, of those endless wheatfields, of northern Europe. She would be a hundred years old now (she had her last child when she was nearly forty). Good student. Scholarship student—like me, later on—she had studied education. At twenty-five, she went to Indochina—it must have been between 1905 and 1910. And there, in the villages of the bush, she taught French and arithmetic to little Annamites. In that era piracy was prevalent in Indochina, as were leprosy, hunger and cholera. Nothing stopped Mother; she spoke of her youth over there as a period of happiness. Then she was married and three children followed. When I think about her now, it's under her maiden name that I see her: Marie Legrand.

One grandfather was Spanish, however; that is why Marie had such black hair with the eyes of a blond: limpid, green. Widowed while still young—she must have been forty-one years old—with three children and her little job, she lived in almost constant poverty. I also see her as a Vietnamese peasant, a hobo of the rice paddies. Stubborn. Crazy about her children. Martyr to our love. Because, of course, she thought it indispensable to get an education, and that stable employment could alleviate life's misfortunes. I see her finally as the first good luck of our childhood: this woman who detested art in all its forms, who never read anything, who never went to the theater or the cinema—a kind of virgin land. We were born of that land. No, I never had a mother who loved painting or art. Nothing was "delightful" for my mother, nor "beautiful," nor "interesting." Nothing but the adventure of daily life, work, food, sleep, and the love of her three *gnos*.[1] Surely,

---

1. Children, in Vietnamese

I never met anyone after who made each day such a violent novelty.

When I wrote the text for *Whole Days in the Trees*, it seemed to me that this piece of writing—yes, I believed it—referred only to the love of the mother for her son: a wild love, an oceanic movement that swallows everything in its depths. I think now that if this aspect remains important in the play, another took its place beside it, that is, the relationship between the two women, the mother and the little whore, the son's friend, Marcelle. And that their common knowledge of Jacques, the loved son, brings them closer despite the social differences—differences apparently impossible to surmount—that exist between them. Between the twenty-five-year-old whore and the irreproachable seventy-five-year-old mother. This unpredictable element in the play gave it a renewed, equally unpredictable, youthfulness at the Theatre d'Orsay this winter. It's strange that a text can conceal these values, and that we are prevented from seeing them because of our backwardness with regard to the basic facts of nature, such as Woman, and love.

Other aspects of the play which seemed scandalous to me twenty years ago—that the son does not work, and that he plays baccarat—don't shock me at all anymore. Even that he steals from his mother no longer scandalizes me as much as it did during my childhood. The scandal has been displaced. It is no longer the brutality of the son toward Marcelle that shocks me, nor the fact that she, Marcelle, tolerates it. It would take only a word that she doesn't utter or that she says only at the end of the play to make him give up this way of speaking. The son appears to me to be lonelier than the woman. With the change in morals—the fantastic change that has taken place in the last ten years—the son is more likable to me than before. He is alone. He is no longer young. He still has the mother that he had at twenty. This mother who preferred him to everything, to us, to everyone. And he, an innocent subject of the fantastic fascination that he exercises over her, hopes she will die so he can stop being preferred to anyone else, so he can sink down into a common fate, the common abyss of the world's orphans.

When I had published the book, I went to see my mother in

that last house that she bought on the banks of the Loire. My mother received me, alone, in bed, dressed in black, as if in mourning again, and she refused to speak to me, to kiss me. She told me simply that she did not understand how I could invent a story as unfounded as the son's in *Whole Days in the Trees*. She added that she was sure she had been fair to her children and that she had made an equal sacrifice for each one. I tried to explain to her that the preference one had for a child might be expressed in almost imperceptible, infinitesimal details, and even if the mother was in no way responsible for it, this different degree of love was experienced as a misfortune by the children who were less well-loved. My mother did not listen and she did not understand what I said to her. I left her on her martyr-mother's bed after she told me how much she deplored my writing books instead of being in business or returning to northern Europe. Her remarks about business are recorded word for word in the film.

No, she did not die after her return from this last visit to her son, her last trip to Europe. She died much later, driven by war, far from this Indochina which became her native land. Alone, at the age of eighty. She meant to call out for my brother with her last words. She craved only a single presence, her son's. I was in the room, I saw them embrace, crying, in despair at having to separate. They did not see me.

Translated by Edith Cohen

Marguerite Duras, seventeen years old.
Sadec (Cochinchine)

Destroy, She Said (C. J. Mascolo)

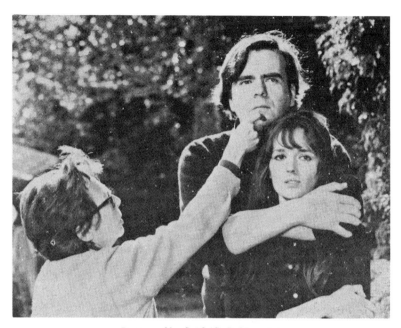

Destroy, She Said (C. J. Mascolo)

Jaune le soleil (C. J. Mascolo)

Nathalie Granger (C. J. Mascolo)

Nathalie Granger (C. J. Mascolo)

Nathalie Granger (C. J. Mascolo)

India Song (C. J. Mascolo)

Son nom de Venise dans Calcutta désert
(Her Venetian Name in Deserted Calcutta)

Son nom de Venise dans Calcutta désert
(Her Venetian Name in Deserted Calcutta)

Le Camion
(The Truck)

Le Camion
(The Truck)

BAXTER, VERA BAXTER
Marguerite Duras

A thousand years ago, they say, in the forests that border the Atlantic, there were women whose husbands were far away, almost always in feudal wars or on a crusade, and sometimes, for months, they were alone in their huts in the middle of the forests, waiting for them. And it was in this way that they began to talk to the trees, to the sea, to the animals of the forest. They were called sorceresses, and were burned.

One of them was named Vera Baxter.

Vera Baxter had just finished boarding school when she married Jean Baxter. He was a friend of her brothers, she had always known him. She was twenty years old.

There was an eighteen-year interval between the time of the marriage and the film. She had three children. At Christine's birth, Jean Baxter lost all his money for the first time. When Mark was born, the money was recovered. Only to disappear again. Then, to come back once more.

At the exact time of the film, the Baxter's have money. A lot of it. Enough to pay a million for a summer villa for the month of August. Vera Baxter is thirty-eight years old.

You could say that Vera Baxter's life, until then, has been riddled with numbers and dates, with numbered and dated reference points. And considering her repertoire of habitual activities, you could go so far as to say that her existence can only be translated into terms of financial balance sheets.

Indeed, nothing has happened to Vera Baxter except to have loved her husband faithfully for eighteen years. To some, the event, here, is this continuance itself. To others, it is the immorality of that love for a man who Vera Baxter herself tells us is "ordinary, without imagination," a patent thief, a gambler, a womanizer, who has nothing else, she says, nothing but this money. But, she adds, *he knows it.* He has this attribute, he knows this about himself.

Before the film, it's Jean Baxter who has brought inevitable desire from the outside back to the couple. Up to now, he alone brought back the refreshing desire of novelty and nourished the marriage with it—it was this method, according to secret ways which defy all analysis, that he used most often.

She never goes outside. No.

She stays at home with the children, maids and housekeepers. Undoubtedly, it is to these companions that she owes her simple, laborious speech that seems almost torn out of her, and her intractability, the difficulty she has in rousing herself from silence.

Vera Baxter has often waited in her apartment on Malesherbes or in Passy. Because he often went off with women he met, and who, each time, he thought were the most important in his life. Each time he left without giving notice. And each time she waited in fear. Until, she says, after a few days, sometimes three, sometimes four, he began to telephone again. On those occasions the permanence of the couple always manifested itself. When he went away, Jean Baxter sent checks to his wife, like others send false telegrams or untruthful letters. Never did he forget to send the signal that the marriage continued in some way: money. Just money.

Of course, we are confining ourselves here to the institutional appearances of marriage. We will never try to penetrate the economic closed places of its continuance.

The Baxter home is to be shunned by anyone who thinks or speaks of passion. Here, nothing heroic, exemplary or clear happens. Nothing. Nothing but this uniform continuance that leads straight to death. Continuance, unconscious of itself. Immobile. Joining the common grave of passion and silence. A silence never named. Passion never named, all the more *true to life* because it feels guilty, threatened by the couple's morality which prevails over it—a morality decreed by what is outside of passion—and based on sterility itself: a deprivation so mad that it drives her to love forever.

I don't know who Vera Baxter is, she who, afflicted with fidelity, lives passion like others do crime, and who knows she is judged a traitor to a theoretical and prevailing liberty by the naive fascism of a new liberating morality.

I don't judge her. I believe I have not judged her.

An ending is needed. I still believe it. One day, Jean Baxter wants others besides himself to approach his wife's body, wants it to be shared, cast out of marriage, into the street, surrendered to others, known, so that others will know it as he does, through desire, the body's only voice. He wants Vera Baxter's desire to spread, to flow out beyond the couple and to return to it, charged with her casual experience. He wants them to come together again in some way through separation itself—as if they were separable—in a contradictory pain, invented by him. He invents, then, the pain of being left by Vera Baxter, his wife.

Vera Baxter is not beautiful. She is a woman who keeps quiet, whom one doesn't *see*, who is incapable of making an effort to please, to be present. And so, Jean Baxter finds himself bound to go through with the sale of his wife so she will be unfaithful to him. He has the means to do it. He does it. He sells her for a great deal of money. The sum corresponds to the rental of a summer villa. The price is intriguing. Why does this woman you don't see cost so much. That's what makes it work. And Vera Baxter becomes adulterous at her husband's command. "Nothing was said before. Nothing will be said afterwards."

LE CAMION
(The Truck)
Joy: We Believe: We Believe Nothing Anymore

It is not worth the trouble to create a cinema of socialist hope for ourselves. Or capitalist hope. No longer worth the trouble to make films about justice to come—social, fiscal, or any other kind. About work. About merit. About women. About young people. The Portuguese. The citizens of Mali. Intellectuals. The Senegalese. No longer worth it to create a cinema about fear. Or revolution. About the dictatorship of the proletariat. Liberty. About your bugaboos. About love. It's no longer worth it.

It's no longer worth the trouble to create a cinema about the cinema. We don't believe anything anymore. We believe. Joy: we believe: nothing anymore. We believe nothing anymore.

No longer worth creating your cinema. Not worth it. We should create a cinema of our knowledge of that—that it's not worth the trouble.

Let the cinema go to ruin, it's the only cinema. Let the world go to its ruin; the fact that it's going to its ruin is the only politics.

Cinema impedes the text, strikes down its progeny—the imaginary—with death.

That is its real strength, to close off, to impede the imaginary.

This impeding, this closing off, is called film. Good or bad, sublime or execrable, film represents this definitive standstill. The fixing of representation, once and for all, forever.

Cinema knows it. It has never been able to replace the text.

Nevertheless, it tries to replace it.

It knows that the text alone is the unlimited image-bearer. But it can't go back to the text again. It doesn't know how to return. It no longer knows the way to the forest, no longer knows how to return to the unlimited potential of the text, to its illimitable proliferation of images.

The cinema is frightened, it fights, struggles; it is out of breath trying to find some other means than language to respond to the growing intelligence of the spectator, to seize him and swallow him up in its movie houses, so he'll consume more of its product.

That's evident. The cinema already sees before it the desert of the cinema. Cinema—opulent, a millionaire, with financial means that rival petroleum transactions and electoral campaigns—tries to recover the spectator.

Films bathe either in beauty or in crime, blood, murders, the beatific, proletarian exoticism, Proust, Balzac, financial scandals, the patience of peoples, the flourishing of hunger.

In vain.

Cinema is no longer able to respond to its audiences' growing thirst for knowledge.

What the cinema doesn't know is that what's happening outside the cinema corresponds to what's happening in it.

That is, even if it is a millionaire, cinema cannot make up for the knowledge that the audience has of how films are made.

Doesn't know that from now on, the fabulous disproportion between the cinema's means and its enterprise will strike dead the product that comes from it.

That it doesn't matter.

That the making of the film is already the film.

Refusal becomes indivisible and total. The spectator stays away from the movies more and more, doesn't go into the theater any more. He knows ahead of time that the product offered to him is tied up in millions, bastardized, polluted by the very conditions of its manufacture.

This refusal knows what it is, it comes out of being asphyxiated by militant orders from all sides. It is liberated.

The movie goer has stopped breaking windows. He walks right by.

He stays on the street rather than go inside.

That's all.

The miserable masses, sunk in complacency, will still go to the theater, but only they alone will go from now on.

They'll put up with a film that has no future, that leaves no trace. A stone in a well.

A lot of people left the cinema long ago.

That is why it still goes on.

I don't know where I'm going in *Le Camion*. The woman in the truck doesn't know either. And it doesn't matter to either of us. I didn't know anything about this woman. Nothing except this: I knew there was a woman at a bend in the road. I saw this road near the English Channel, on the way to the Hague, and she was waiting for a truck, and for me. Just that, for several weeks. I didn't work on the text. I knew that whatever it was, it would be swept away in the shooting. That the woman and the text would not coincide prior to the film. That the woman would only begin to exist with the film, simultaneously with the film's unfolding.

More than that, I knew that the woman needed the film in order to begin to exist. Before the film, I see only her waiting. I know how to love her. I am attracted to her. As for her, no, she is turned away, attracted to the outside. She doesn't know I love her, doesn't know how to be loved; she is ignorant of the love she can inspire. Turned away, she looks. I am turned toward her, look at her. Both of us telescoped, facing out. It's through her that I see. Through her that I take the outside and swallow it up in myself. I love her. She doesn't know me, always turned outward. I shift my gaze. I look at what she looks at; it grows lighter and lighter. I don't see her, I still don't see her face. When the film ends, I've never seen her face. But what she was looking at dazzled me: the film.

In *India Song* I tried to make the love story overflow its terrain. Through Michael Richardson, Anne-Marie Stretter loves *Calcutta* completely.

In *Le Camion*, the story, the pretext for talking about love, has disappeared. The woman in *Le Camion* lives a love of a general kind. She doesn't know how to live it. Turned completely outward, she is in the process of losing her identity. Not only does she not know who she is anymore, she searches everywhere for who she might be. In *Le Camion*, no reference to a possible identity remains but the *practice* of hitchhiking. She is nothing more than a hitchhiker. In the same way she first appeared to me, I see her disappear in another vehicle, I see her leave me. She stays like that, annulled somewhere in a perpetual state of waiting with the perpetual wish to be everything at once. That attraction of hers to everything is an attraction I call love.

100

The woman of *Le Camion* is no longer bored. She doesn't look for any *meaning* in her life. I discover in her a joy of existing *without* a need to search for meaning. A real regression, ongoing, fundamental. The only recourse here being the decisive knowledge of the nonexistence of any recourse whatsoever.

THE PATH OF JOYFUL DESPAIR
An interview with Marguerite Duras
by Claire Devarrieux

How can one conceive of a film which is based only on words?

Le Camion is not based only on words, there is someone who reads, and someone who listens. The truck on a road is an image, it's the image. It could not have been done as theater. *Le Camion* is not acted, it is read and it was not rehearsed. If it had been it would have been another film.

I don't know if one can speak of directing or even of editing in *Le Camion*, but perhaps only of putting into place. In the chain of representation there is a blank interval: in general, a text is learned, acted, staged. This one is read. And here is the uncertainty. I don't know what happened. I did it by instinct and afterwards discovered that representation had been eliminated. *Le Camion* is nothing but representation of reading itself. And then there is the truck, a constant, always identical to itself, which extends across the screen like a musical staff.

I read *Le Camion* as I hear the writing take place. Before its projection on the page, one hears it. Before a sentence emerges, it is heard. I stay in that place, nearest to the inner voice. In general, writing is projected on the page and then apprehended by another person. That is theater. In *Le Camion*, that doesn't happen. You don't descend toward the fragmentation of the text. Reading makes you rise toward it, toward the place where it's not yet spoken. In a personal relationship, in life, there's spontaneous speech, and that's that, you can't retrieve that in film or in the theater. There's a kind of passage in the activating of a script that wears it out, makes it age. In *Le Camion*, no one ever heard the script except for me, because I wrote it. Of course, that's a very big risk. *Le Camion* is that risk.

It is an approximate and interchangeable script for the most part. There's that, which counts for a lot. At any time, I allowed myself to change everything. The film was written at the same time it's shot. *Le Camion* is that, too. The film is endangered at every moment, the sequence was not written down in advance and even now the film is in danger of not existing. Even when I see it, I tell myself it's going to end, it's in danger of breaking down. I've never made a film in such doubt. Instead of this doubt being sterile, it meant greater freedom for Gerard Depardieu and me. We didn't know where we were going, there's a complete virtuality at the beginning and the end of this story that never takes place, that's stopped before it happens. Perhaps a question about the stopping of the story is in order.

The responsibility for stopping the story lies with the driver. He refuses it. The driver is also the spectator. The woman often responds to the spectator through him. Their disparity is the subject of the film—how the woman responds to the spectators was very striking at Cannes. The cabin of the truck is the movie theater. They're all locked up together in the same place, the spectator and the film, the woman and the driver.

Let's return to representation.

In a theatrical and cinematographic representation, who speaks? I do not believe it's the author. It's the director and actor. They take charge of the script. As soon as it is put into writing, the written text, the book is closed. At this point in our journey, no one knows the scope of the text except the author. No one has translated it yet. The author's working process is completely solitary, not transmittable through staging and actors. They learn the script, translate it. Either the author recognizes the work or is horrified. That has happened to me. I had to go back to the book to find my text again. In *Le Camion* these intermediaries no longer exist.

It is when a script is performed that we're furthest from the author. Even when I directed my own scripts, it happened to me—except in *India Song*. In *India Song* the actors proposed characters but didn't embody them. "Off screen" is still the place of writing. Delphine Seyrig's fantastic performance in *India Song* came about because she never presents herself as someone named Anne-Marie Stretter but as her far-off, contestable double, as if uninhabited, and as if she never regarded this role as an emptiness to be enacted; but on the contrary, as though her reference to the written Anne-Marie Stretter remained intact. As for my other films, some even-

103

ings after a shoot, I had the sense I had lost my text. I was in despair. Its undefined virtuality was destroyed, it left its written
form to end up as a sort of definitive utterance. To be completely
honest, I have always suffered from this transformation, this shat-
tering of the text's obscurities; it's because of that I made *Le Camion*. The actors were not the problem. I had the best, Claudine
Gabey for Vera Baxter. No, it's as if my writing were something
clandestine and once it was taken over through speech, the written
text came through.

But then, what about Le Camion?

An actor confronts the text and takes hold of it. He is never
behind it. When I read there is an exact correspondence with my
text. In *Le Camion* there is no staging of the reading, there is just
reading and that's what I try to express, what I hear when I write.
It's what I've always called the interior voice. If people reject *Le '
Camion*, it's because they reject the nature of the text as it's read.
So then it's a total rejection.

Because of the way the text and narration is taken over by the
actors and directors, I can't go to the movies any more. It is difficult to talk about. There are a thousand years of theater behind us.
Millennia of power behind us.

Is it the same power?

It's power, yes. There's no difference between what happens
every evening on television and commercial films. No difference
between the politicians in power and those in the opposition, and
the way actors are obliged to act. Sometimes the play-acting ends.
That's very rare. It happened when Mendès France spoke the other
day. It was completely staggering, someone who didn't lie. The
others are representatives, they act. Actors and politicians are del-
egates, they're no longer themselves, they sell their merchandise.
A good actor is one who sells the best; he is the best spokesman for
his merchandise. Some are not charlatans; they, like Mendès
France, are in some way distracted from representation.

Film and politics are alike. Both depend on spectacle. Cinema comes from spectacle. Politics is a spectacle, diverting or not,
and for many it's just entertainment. There is the same hiatus at
the outset—I was going to say the same lie—both in political rep-

resentation and commercial cinematographic representation.

To speak in the name of established power, or in the name of a power to come is the same thing. In political discourse, the capacity for error is completely banished. They all have the ideal solution, they're the saviors, the perfect guardians of what I call the political solution. They all base what they say on a radical solution, on power. I find this affirmation in classical actors, in theatrical declamation, in the purely psychological technique of film actors. It is they who possess the truth of the role, they who possess the truth of the future. And we can't take that any more.

Perhaps we need to abandon this kind of fixed, rationalist, European habit of needing a political solution. This taking charge of the individual, by any State, no matter which, is the trap. And the terror. The fear people have of being left to themselves is a learned fear. They see the solution in a political program, in a party solution. They prefer any political program to the absence of a program, any kind of direction, debauchery, or political swindling to the absence of a solution. The solution of politicians in or out of power is exactly the same.

Cinema is everywhere; and the theater, too, belongs to the opposition as well as the majority. Perhaps that's what's finished. The political lie is apparent everywhere; why shouldn't the journalistic and cinematographic lie be denounced in the same way?

The woman of Le Camion *says, "Let the world go to its ruin, that's the only politics." What does that mean?*

There's an ambiguity: "Let the world go to its ruin is the only politics" is not a profession of anarchist faith. It's an option. To drop the political idea, political exigencies. I prefer a vacuum, a real vacuum to the kind of junk yard, the giant garbage can of every 20th-century ideology. I prefer an absence of the State, no power at all, to the deceitful, false, lying propositions about the possibility of a democratic state, of the socialist road, while everything contradicts this possibility. My political despair, which is everyone's, becomes a commonplace in the cinema. Films bathe in political despair, from Italian neorealism to American necrorealism. We're calm, everybody's desperate, it gets to be commonplace. It becomes an addiction to the past, the most dangerous kind. I believe we must leave all that. We've been taught from childhood

105

on that all our efforts ought to go toward finding the meaning of the life we lead, of the one offered to us. We must find a way out. And it should be joyful.

And how can it be joyful?

It hinges on the inculcated fear of something missing, of disorder. We need to overcome that. When someone no longer has this fear, he does harm to the powers that be. There is a complete equivalence among things. The individual can only find his own way out by adopting a fundamental indifference to what is proposed, to political matters, or to business affairs. Fear must diminish: every time it is there, power is in control. The link between fear and power is direct.

The driver of *Le Camion* adheres forever to a solution proposed by the French Communist Party. He kills all spirit of freedom in himself. How do you get to that point, to accepting an assumption of responsibility by political and union organizations? It is this problem of the proletariat that's posed in the film. The truck driver is defined by absolute alienation. How did the enlisted working class get to that point? To the rejection of the spirit of May, 1968? To this fundamental refusal of life, of living? To be an official member of the French Communist Party is to be apolitical. I don't know what the future of cinema is and I don't give a damn. If I had the least idea about the future, I would still perform an act of power. Power would still be the basis of my judgement. *Le Camion* is a cinematic act.

And the woman of Le Camion?

This woman without a face, without an identity, degraded in class, who may even be an escapee from a mental institution, who claims she's the mother of all the dead Jewish children at Auschwitz, or believes she is Portuguese or an Arab, or from Mali, who reinvents everything she's been taught—this woman, for me, is open to the future. If she's mad, so much the better, let everyone be mad like her. Mad, I'm using it in the sense that the spectator would understand it. The spectator needs to recognize before judging. If he doesn't recognize in this woman her attraction to all oppressions, an attraction I call love, I can't do anything for him to make him join her. The spectator is challenged. Like the militant. I

106

challenge his responsibility, the responsibility of the spectator class as well as the working class. For decades now there's the same immobility, the same breakdown. It's the spectator who will put himself into the hands of all powers, of all the ideologies. His dependency, his fantastic equation of submission is what defines him.

Who is Vera Baxter in the film?

She is an infernal woman, prey to her fidelity. She is perhaps a desperate case. What I know, what we all know is that this case exists. She's infernal because of her unequivocal vocation to marriage, to fidelity. But if I'm not mistaken, isn't desire the desire of a single being? Isn't desire the opposite of the scattering of desire?

What I know about Vera Baxter is that her existence has a completely reassuring, normal appearance, and that she should be recognized everywhere as the perfect woman and mother—that's what scares me. It's not the woman of *Le Camion* who frightens me, it's Vera Baxter. The woman in *Le Camion* is not circumscribed by any identity. She's broken with all possible identities, she is nothing more than a hitchhiker. Some have a theoretical practice, Marxist or some other, at their disposal. She has only the practice of hitchhiking.

Before the film starts, Vera Baxter is apparently without recourse. She is a victim of love, if you will. In the film, Vera Baxter meets with an accident. That of desire. The fact that Jean Baxter paid a stranger so his wife can stop being faithful to him also depends on desire. The paid adultery of Vera Baxter was supposed to make profitable the couple's desire. But the expected result was not produced. Vera Baxter, let loose into prostitution, paid or not, will never go back to Jean Baxter. She may die of it. I mean, she will die of no longer loving the same man until death do them part. I think she wants to kill herself simply because it's no longer possible to love the same man all her life. That is probably the archaism of Vera Baxter. This woman of the medieval forests: today there are millions let loose in the world. I think that if Vera Baxter met the woman of *Le Camion* she would be afraid of her, but wouldn't relegate her to the political or mental categories that the driver of *Le Camion* does. What they undoubtedly, irremediably have in common is love. Vera Baxter's love for her children, her husband—we've heard about that for a long time. The love of the woman in *Le Camion*—formless, anarchic, dangerous—we know less well. Loving a child or loving all children, alive or dead, comes together somewhere. Loving a criminal, lower class but humble, or an honest man who believes himself to be so, also comes to the same thing.

Translated by Edith Cohen

"AN ACT AGAINST ALL POWER"
An interview with Marguerite Duras
by Jacques Grant and Jacques Frenais

You've seen *Vera Baxter.*

Yes, of course.

I spoiled it. I'm going to publish the real script of *Vera Baxter* in which the unknown person who arrives at Vera Baxter's is a man. Because of certain circumstances that I allowed to affect me, I replaced the man with a woman.

What were the circumstances?

The women's movement and all that. It seemed to me if there was another story with a man, it would work against the love story between Vera Baxter and her husband, and at the last minute I changed everything. I put in another woman. And, in my view, it doesn't work because they spend their time avoiding each other in the film.

In fact, this ties in strangely with what is written about the film in the review where they talk about a police-like relationship between the women. That's exactly it: Vera Baxter feels she is being interrogated and avoids her.

I wouldn't say police-like. In theory it's a troubled relationship, an attraction. In the script it's the word "Baxter" that makes him come, a little like the word "Stein" in *Destroy.* The word "Baxter" begins to act on the unknown man; it is completely a question of desire, whereas in the film it's to some degree, if one can speak of it that way, a question of militancy. She almost goes to the aid of the other woman, whereas it was desire that blazed up at the name of "Baxter," at the sound of these two words—Vera Baxter. I believed I could go beyond homosexuality, that forbidden territory, that kind of difference. In matters like these, you should be faithful to yourself.

With Delphine, they avoid each other, don't touch, speak from a distance. They could come together. Hostility to that degree signifies something, perhaps. In any case it's not what I wanted. If there had been a man instead of the woman visitor, the fact that they avoid each other as they do would be inscribed directly in the cleavage of a desire to come, a positive relationship. While with the two women, it has a completely different meaning. They approach each other for no reason at all.

It isn't necessarily perceived like that, of course; it's for myself that I ruined it. For example, a physical relationship exists completely between Vera Baxter and the first woman, Monique Combes, when they talk near the bed, when they talk about the man, Jean Baxter. It is afterwards, when the action is gratuitous, in a kind of physical pseudo-community of women, that it doesn't work, simply because it doesn't matter to me.

But does it concern you in the first case?

No, because there is a man between them. They have that in common, knowing Jean Baxter.

But you didn't really intend to put this desire in. Aren't you saying that after the fact, out of regret that there isn't any?

No, I thought I could do without it. I thought the fact of belonging to the same gender could fill in a lot of things because of the man's absence. But it isn't so.

Everything you say allows us to suppose that the relationship formed between the woman visitor and Vera Baxter surprises you. Goes beyond your expectations or stops short of them.

But when I say that, don't you realize something?

What's very important about Vera Baxter *is that it's a terrifying film.*

Vera Baxter has almost lost the power of speech. She's a woman who has spoken to children, to maids, to charwomen for eighteen years, and to draw her out of silence is very painful. She has a laborious, almost painful, unpleasant way of speaking and this is what I like in *Vera Baxter*, this kind of archaism, Vera Baxter's archaic quality. That's the entirely positive side, the choice of Claudine Gabay.

That's what's frightening, isn't it? This woman has a kind of

110

singular vocation, in this marriage, and the prostitution latent in all these women, in all bourgeois women, is erased, disappears. Unless something else you're thinking of is terrifying in *Vera Baxter*.

It's astonishing to hear you talk about Vera Baxter as if she had a theoretical existence, as if she were someone you could theorize about. All through the first part of the film, one wonders if she exists, and then in the second part of the film, when she is confronted by these two women, and in particular by Delphine Seyrig, Vera Baxter seems attracted, in a mechanical way, to the two women—that is, one wonders if Vera Baxter isn't Delphine Seyrig.

I can't see *Vera Baxter* without asking myself that question. Originally there weren't two people. Vera Baxter remained in her impregnable solitude. No one came.

And Delphine Seyrig draws out part of Vera Baxter's existence.

Yes, you're right. But I don't see that as a division between someone who eats and someone who is eaten.

And you, without a man's being there, you're still able to see Vera Baxter's body. For myself, without a man to look, I'm unable to see Vera Baxter's body.

That's why when we spoke of attraction it was not a question of the consumable but of the cinematographic. Which would explain why you felt obliged to put in those very beautiful inserts of the nude body. One wonders, "how did this necessity arise?"

I had to make it exist somewhere.

Was it because of the very strong presence of the man in Le Camion, *so close to you in time?*

It was latent for a long time. There was something that didn't work in *Baxter*. When I was editing *Le Camion* I understood that it was ruined. That's where I am: I'm going to publish the script.

One thing that strikes me, à propos of Vera Baxter *and* Le Camion *is that these two films take place in what people generally call real time while you only approximate it in your other films.*

I didn't do it on purpose. I'm thinking now about what you

111

say. There is no narrative outside of the narrative that's seen.

It doesn't seem to interest you to section off lives, to represent people at different moments of their lives. You seem entirely opposed to a naturalist aesthetic.

Cinema has never been equal to the fundamental futility of life. The viewer wants someone to tell him a story about this life in such a way that the inanity on which the story is based is never apparent. It has to be far away, camouflaged, inaccessible, separate. But progress has come, terrible and terrifying: the whole Earth is more and more apparent. We know its shape, its dizzying spin. We have seen it from the moon. It's in everyone's imaginary. That Earth, that new Earth and its fundamental futility across the dead planets. I have the impression that I showed in *Le Camion* that there is no more sky above the land we see, just interstellar space, the new sky.

As far as the truck driver is concerned, there is no sense of time, because it never entered his life; and in *Vera Baxter* no sense of continuance in what concerns her life as a woman because we never entered into such a life. *Le Camion* is about an impossible relationship. Therefore the relationship between the two individuals is the subject of the film, the film's psychological subject. But we never infringe on the space of the truck: we're never going to see who she is nor who he is.

In Le Camion, *it is not the relationship that seems impossible. It is the desire to enter into a relationship that appears to be in vain. Because according to the evidence the two people have not received the same treatment. To put it simply, one of the characters is more important than the other one; she reveals herself and that's why it's astonishing to hear you say that no one knows who she is. In any case, who she is, much more than who he is.*

She offers herself.

She offers herself to him; she invents him as a target. The difference between Le Camion *and the other films is simply you.*

Not always. We don't always speak from the same place. Sometimes it gets mixed up. I agree, the two places are confused, they slide toward each other, her place and the place from which I speak.

I say an "impossible relationship," and you say a "relationship refused."

No, not refused.

Rejected then. The proletariat does not want to talk to this woman.

This woman is the artisan of her own proletariat, she made her own proletariat.

Oh no! It is the proletariat who answers to the name. It's the proletariat that wants to be answerable to a class, to the working class. Whereas she doesn't depend on any class. She is perhaps like that, an animal looking for a class, I'd say, not a social class, an animal class. She is looking for some sort of well-being. It's this attraction to the whole that I call "love." When she says she remembers these houses, this color, this cold, these people—it is like an utopian, imaginary attachment to poverty. And he answers from a completely workerist, retrogressive dialectic.

. . . Through his voice to her . . .

. . . He says to her: you couldn't have ever lived here, you lie; no one has ever lived here, you lie. Now, she thinks she recognizes all that. From an imaginary viewpoint she knows poverty, the intolerable, the cold and all that. And he puts her down immediately. She says: "I know . . . but this is the way that I love." And he says to her again, "You lie," and she keeps quiet. Do you recognize this sanction? I know it very well.

One of the constants, one of the facts of this world, is the existence, the recognition of a proletarian class and the image one associates with it.

That's a superficial approach, a simplification that he wants to maintain. Of course it's true she didn't live in that world; we see houses in disrepair, houses under construction, Portuguese hovels, S. Quentin-en-Yvelins (financing scandals); she says that she recognizes all that—she's a little unbalanced. He probably begins to listen then. How can this encroachment from class to class exist, how can this class impenetrability be wiped out, and how can a woman who is declassé slip into another status—that must intrigue him. But he doesn't have the ability to listen deeply, he can't listen at all. He is rotten with orders. Orders are killing him. He has an answer to everything, including her madness—to her love, if you will. It's completely a speech of love I'm talking about there, and he passes judgement on it as he would a logical argument.

He is defined in relation to her madness . . .

The guy in the truck has, is only meant to have, only one definition. He has two strict allegiances: to a very scholarly syndicalism, and a pseudo-revolutionary Stalinist party. And outside of that, beyond these two affiliations, he is nothing, he is in fact without an answer. He tries the whole time to bring the woman into his world which is a closed place, a place of asphyxiation. I know this world, I was in the French Communist Party for eight years. But *Le Camion* may not be about that.

You said earlier that Vera Baxter *ends when the man enters and, after seeing her, his fascination for the name "Vera Baxter" is transformed into a fascination for Vera Baxter's body.*

For the body of woman in general.

In Le Camion, *as soon as she is no longer in charge, the woman no longer has a body, she has nothing more than speech and, from that moment, the man doesn't desire her; he rejects her, that is, she makes him afraid. Do you see something in the difference between an approach through the body and an approach through speech? How a woman manifested through speech could be terrifying to a man?*

I'm afraid not. That's a pertinent question. But I as a woman and you as a man—that's where we are closed off to each other. A man's approach, whether through speech or the body, is identical to me.

And, moreover, with regard to the interrogatory relationship, the police-like relation between the women in *Vera Baxter* of which we spoke earlier, I can explain it. Vera Baxter is not capable of speaking about herself. She doesn't know how to be alert, inter-

114

esting; she is extremely backward. So you have to pull things out of her. This is definitively an intrinsic part of Vera Baxter. She has never had the dimension of presence, of being there. Who has ever asked Vera Baxter to talk about her life, about herself? No one. She's in a place where you don't speak freely, unconventionally, don't volunteer a word.

But in *Le Camion* there is de facto discrimination. For the truck driver it is, above all, a woman who speaks. The first hint refers to that.

The second, to her being an older woman.

Yes, discrimination is important in its multiplicity.

In its plural.

But it seems particularly interesting when one remembers that the woman's speech is suddenly very invasive and perhaps very dangerous. You can ask yourself how and why. It's true that it's exasperating to hear a woman talk.

You are sure of what you're saying?

Yes, it's something that makes your hair stand on end. It's very disturbing. Whereas her body isn't. It's proven iconographically.

Yes. Perhaps because the woman in the truck has gone beyond the functional age, I mean the conventional age of exchange. But transgression still works there. Gerard Depardieu and I are both *in a nocturnal place and that, in broad daylight.* It's a movie theater as well as a bordello. Nothing apparently happens for someone *who sees nothing:* the text is, in itself, desire and consummation of desire. Why refuse the cinema what happens every day throughout the entire world in letters, speeches, and telephone calls? If you could manage to get hold of the wild network of the telephone at night, you would be witness to a dazzling display of desire. There, one calls for the sake of calling. There, words alone are themselves the support of desire. Perhaps I have never written as close to desire as in those silences between Gerard Depardieu and me in the text of *Le Camion.*

Wouldn't Le Camion *be in fact the story of a woman who*

wants to hear a man talk, hear men talk? Because men don't talk in an audible fashion any more.

No, what she wants to do is to speak, to write. She isn't waiting for an answer. Think about writing's two parallel acts. I know there is nothing closer to this woman than the act of writing. To write is also to speak well in this way, without an immediate interlocutor; it's the stage between writing something and its publication. If there is a response, that's good. If there is no response, she closes her eyes, she sings. It's been a long time since I've found characters so . . . fraternal.

There's a phenomenon of deafness, of blindness in men. During my eight years in the Party, I was taught to look down on people who were declassé, taught to scorn them. If you are even a little weak, it's very difficult to cleanse yourself of this abhorrence. In some way I'd become a scoundrel as well as an excellent militant. What I'm describing here is an absolutely classical everyday experience. To belong to the Party you have to be weak somewhere, be autistic.

There are, moreover, on the formal plane, a fair number of connotations of autism in the film: the truck that travels in a circle.

Above all else, I see in the phenomenon of militantism an autistic phenomenon. You entrust yourself to a machine that carries you along. If I make a connection between my conjugal experience, the common human life, and life held up by the Party, I see at the bottom of all that the same neurosis of even more; it's almost psychotic, the wish to be irresponsible.

But in the act of writing or of making films as you've just described it, there is also an autistic reality: if there's no response, she closes her eyes. As far as I'm concerned, I can only write because it becomes public.

In fact the whole film expresses the proletarian dream. From the moment you choose a truck driver the specific desire of the man is intrinsically inscribed in the film in a proletarian man. And then there is the choice of Depardieu who projects a very typical image of the proletariat.

I am a communist. I live a derided, butchered communism. I

would never have thought to put this woman who confronts the bewilderment of love, of universal love, in anything but the working class, the class that's most important to me. It wasn't by chance.

The class that's most important to you and the one that makes you afraid?

It doesn't make me afraid, otherwise I wouldn't accuse it. I question its responsibility. We question the responsibility of intellectuals, philosophers, capitalism, the bourgeoisie; we never question the responsibility of the proletariat. In May, 1968, information was as widely diffused as could be. There was the possibility for all, for every proletarian to inform himself; but no one sought information from the outside. They all obeyed orders. I can't forget that. Before '68 I would not have been able, would not have dared talk that way. Now I can see a worker and talk to him like an equal. Recently I had dealings with a Portuguese worker who thought it was all right to be constructing houses that looked alike. I was able to tell him that people who have those things built and think they are all right are shit. When I was secretary in the cell, I would never have dared to attack an immigrant worker straight-on.

In Le Camion *you don't speak for any one. As filmmaker, you are the passenger who, as you said earlier, knows the difference between the unendurable and the imaginary. The film's entire construction—the place you speak from, the place where you are calmly seated—is your speech alone.* Le Camion *is your own discourse.*
To be more exact we can't accept Le Camion *as a film that allows you to question your own contestation—the responsibility of the proletariat—which the film shows only in flashes.*

I agree. It's not the major subject.

The main subject is you speaking. You holding forth. And your discourse is just that.

You're saying that there is a game that is not played. There is no longer any distance then between the speaker and the person represented. Therefore there's no game.

Not only is there no game, there's no representation that per-

117

mits catharsis of what's evoked. That is the essential quality and force of the film. On the other hand, where does its efficacy lie? Which of your ideas turns ours around? But that's no doubt the problem, isn't it?

Because speech is not a weapon. It's a place. And I think that even the form of *Le Camion* is more effective than its detail.

For the first time in one of your films the place from which you speak, the source of the film, is your mouth, your voice.

Therefore it's my liberty.

It's more complicated.

But, I think the film is an open space, free. The cigarettes, the armchair, we take our time. And it doesn't fall apart. If *Le Camion* was really a narrative with logical connections, psychological points, etc., the film would break apart all the time. It is continually being threatened by death. And what makes it hold together, I think that's it, is the notion of the will to speak, of unleashing the will to speak.

Which is not to say that this woman is you. This woman is your discourse, not you. On the other hand, Depardieu is an actor.

No one can be represented, not even me, for the same reason. But here it's plain to see. There is no pretence of representation.

Of a lie. You do not pretend to lie. On the other hand Depardieu makes himself understood very quickly. We say to ourselves, that's not a proletarian. We see right away that we are falling into our own trap because of course he's not a proletarian; he's an actor, he's sitting there at a table, everyone knows him. That's what Le Camion *is for me.*

If I understand correctly, what has changed in relation to other films is the place of narration.

It's speech as the locus of the film.

The locus of the narrative was in its representation, while now it's in the text itself.

So in Vera Baxter *you open the film with your voice and after that you represent something in relation to what is being said.*

There is an essential lack in *Le Camion*. In the representative chain, in the chain of representation, we might even say in the symbolic chain, there is a link that snaps open, there is a blank space.

That's completely evident and rather cruel. Because at no time is there a chance to escape. . . .

To escape it.

Perhaps two or three moments nevertheless, when the truck disappears on the road to the right.

When the truck sees, or when it is seen?

When it is seen. There it's the oasis, the mirage. The lure.

A beginning of representation. The image that would have been seen among others, if the film had been shot. Without it the film would, perhaps, have been unendurable.

In an instant, it became possible for the sea to exist, for someone to be in the truck, for us to arrive at the daughter's house, for the child not to be called Abraham, for him to be sweet, to cry a little, I don't know what else—other things.

Things which were not invented.

People have reproached Le Camion *and its time changes for being fraudulent.*

But that's the whole film. There's a critic on "Telerama" who makes a big mistake. He says, "Depardieu asks, 'Would it be a film?' Marguerite Duras reprimands Depardieu and says to him (severely), "It *is* a film." Now everyone hears a "therefore" between the two phrases: "It would have been a film," *therefore* "it is a film." The supposition, the hypothesis becomes reality: for children the conditional is lucid time, par excellence. I would be a truck is equivalent to being a truck. Note that many grammarians tend to assimilate the conditional with the indicative mode. It is certain that it disturbs classical narration. At the Bachot they would refuse *Le Camion*. From page to page I make grammatical leaps.

119

In Le Camion, *one can say that the form is defined politically as opposed to so-called political films.*

In *Le Camion*, the form has reverted to an impoverished archaic form that kept the text as the only factor to proliferate an image against an image, while *Hands Over the City (Le mani sulla cita)* submits to classic representation. It's an American film based on real Italian events. It's a film that doesn't invent its bases; there is no difference between a love story that takes place in the Michigan area and *Hands Over the City*. It's exactly the same formalism. Except that the form of the American love story is coherent; it doesn't have to invent its form. *Hands Over the City*, yes. I sometimes have the impression that cinema is guarded by a secret police. It is a kind of supermarket kept under guard. Either you get past them or you're not recognized. If you distinguish yourself you're poorly regarded.

Le Camion *is very highly regarded.*

I film with the fundamental suspicion that cinema scarcely exists, compared to what's written.

It's because my cinema scarcely exists as cinema that I can make these films. The type of perfection to which mainstream cinema aspires (in its use of clever technique with the sole aim of maintaining order) is accurately inscribed in its precise adherence to prevailing social codes. We show incest but we cut it into eighty-five splices so that everyone recognizes it but no one witnesses it. Porn cinema shows it. Mainstream cinema can be very clever, but it is rarely intelligent.

There is always the sea in your films.

In *Le Camion* is accompanies the trip. It suggests annihilation, the end of the world.

When you say: "That the world is going to its ruin is the only politics," which leads us to believe that you are not afraid, isn't that a way of reassuring yourself? We are now confronted with the coming to power of the Union of the Left; we catch ourselves wanting it on condition that it would bring about a catastrophe. And that's facile.

What can I say? In fact, the world is already in a catastrophic state. There will always be a political solution and whatever it is will not satisfy us. The governed are always infinitely more advanced than those who govern.

Even the proletariat? And how does it happen that there are people who govern?

They are necessary. What we must fight is Power, all the time. Fight Marxism as a means of power which it, alas, has become—semiotic as well as political power. Marxist semiology has become a phallocratic terror. It's also a factor in holding women back—the fact that they insist on catching up with the semiotic jargon of that whole platform that came along in the Marxist aftermath.

We can no longer be content to look for a political solution, we must not look for a political solution.

In other words, people are becoming indifferent to the kind of panicky rescue of capitalism which we are seeing now.

Yes. It becomes theater. We are governed by a financial oligarchy, that's all there is to it, we know it. Nothing holds together any more. We've been disappointed by democracy, by socialism. There's only utopia that furthers the idea of the Left. The belief in a political solution brought about by a party in power or one that will come to power—that's the great regression today. All we can do to fight against that is to perform free acts. *Le Camion* is a free act, it's an act against all Power. The only way to advance a leftist idea is not to ask if it will succeed; it's to express it in a free act. As I was saying to Anne de Gaspari in *Le Quotidien de Paris*, we must leave this miserable despair behind and get to the point where no longer believing in anything becomes positive. There is a political despair which has become a convention of the cinema from Italian neorealism to the necrorealism of the American type, as in *Clockwork Orange*. Its addiction to the past plays into the hands of all the powers that be. *Le Camion* is an acute form of political despair, acute and joyous.

From In Cinéma 77
(Neauphle-le-Château, June 1977)

HOMAGE TO MARGUERITE DURAS,
on *Le ravissement de Lol V. Stein**

Jacques Lacan

Le ravissement—this word is enigmatic. Does it have an objective or a subjective dimension—is it a ravishing or a being ravished—as determined by Lol V. Stein?

Ravished. We think of the soul, and of the effect wrought by beauty. But we shall free ourselves, as best we can, from this readily available meaning, by means of a symbol.

A woman who ravishes is also the image imposed on us by this wounded figure, exiled from things, whom you dare not touch, but who makes you her prey.

The two movements, however, are knotted together in a cipher that is revealed in a name skillfully crafted in the contour of writing: Lol V. Stein.

Lol V. Stein: paper wings, V, scissors, Stein, stone, in love's guessing game you lose yourself.

One replies: O, open mouth, why do I take three leaps on the water, out of the game of love, where do I plunge?

Such artistry suggests that the ravisher is Marguerite Duras, and we are the ravished. But if, to quicken our steps behind Lol's steps, which resonate through the novel, we were to hear them behind us without having run into anyone, is it then that her creature moves within a space which is doubled; or is it rather that one of us has passed through the other, and which of us, in that case, has let himself be traversed?

Or do we now realize that the cipher is to be calculated in some other way: for to figure it out, one must count *oneself* three.

But let's read.

The scene of which the entire novel is but a recollection describes the enrapturing of two in a dance that fuses them together before the entire ball and under the eyes of Lol, the third, who

---

*Le ravissement de Lol V. Stein was published in America under the title, *The Ravishing of Lol Stein*, Grove Press, 1966.

endures the abduction of her fiancé by a woman who had only suddenly to appear.

And to get at what Lol is seeking from this moment on, must we not have her say, "*Je me deux*," to conjugate, with Apollinaire, "*douloir?*"[1]

But, precisely, she cannot say that she suffers.

Thinking along the lines of some cliché, we might say she is repeating the event. But we should look more closely than this.

This is roughly what we discern in this scene, to which Lol will return many times, where she watches a pair of lovers in whom she has found, as if by chance, a friend who was close to her before the drama, and who helped her even as it unfolded: Tatiana.

This is not the event, but a knot retying itself there. And it is what this knot ties up that actually ravishes—but then again, whom?

The least we can say is that at this point the story puts one character in balance, and not only because Marguerite Duras has invested this character with the narrative voice: the other partner of the couple. His name, Jacques Hold.

Nor is he what he appears to be when I say: the narrative voice. He is, rather, its anguish. Once again the ambiguity returns: is it his anguish, or that of the narrative? He does not, in any case, simply display the machinery, but is in fact one of its mainsprings, and he does not now just how taken up in it he is.

This allows me to introduce Marguerite Duras here, having moreover her consent to do so, as the third ternary, of which one of the terms remains the ravishment of Lol V. Stein caught as an object in her own knot, and in which I myself am the third to propose a ravishment, in my case, a decidedly subjective one.

What I have just described is not a madrigal, but a limit of method, one whose positive and negative value I hope to affirm here. A subject is a scientific *term*, something perfectly calculable, and this reminder of its status should terminate what can only be

---

[1] *Je me deux* is the first person reflexive form of the now archaic French infinitive, meaning to feel sorrow. It means, therefore, "I feel sorrow," but also, read in another way, it can mean literally, "I two myself." No English verb captures the ambiguity of the French; the closest approximation might be, "I am rent," which suggests the splitting of the subject of which Lacan will be speaking. (TN)

called by its name, boorishness: let us say thè pedantry of a certain kind of psychoanalysis. This frivolous aspect of psychoanalysis, to remain sensitive, one hopes, to those who immerse themselves in it, ought to indicate to them that they are sliding towards stupidity; for example, by attributing an author's avowed technique to some neurosis: boorishness. Or again, by showing it to be an explicit adoption of certain mechanisms which would thereby make an unconscious edifice of it: stupidity.

I think that even if I were to hear it from Marguerite Duras herself that, in her entire *oeuvre*, she doesn't know where Lol has come from, and even if I could glean this from the next sentence she says to me, the only advantage that the psychoanalyst has the right to draw from his position, were this then to be recognized as such, is to recall with Freud that in his work the artist always precedes him, and that he does not have to play the psychologist where the artist paves the way for him.

This is precisely what I acknowledge to be the case in the ravishing of Lol V. Stein, where it turns out that Marguerite Duras knows, without me, what I teach.

In this respect, I do not wrong her genius in bringing my critique to bear on the virtue of her talents.

In paying homage to her, all that I shall show is that the practice of the letter converges with the workings of the unconscious.

Let me assure whoever might read these lines by the dimming or rising footlights—indeed, from those future shores where Jean-Louis Barrault, through his *Cahiers*,[2] would harbor the unique conjunction of the theatrical act—that the thread I will be unraveling takes its bearings at every moment, and to the letter, from the ravishing of Lol V. Stein; and furthermore, that work going on today at my school certainly crosses paths with it. Moreover, I do not so much address myself to this reader as I draw upon his inmost being in order to practice the knot I unravel.

This thread is to be picked up in the first scene, where Lol is robbed of her lover; that is to say, it is to be traced in the motif of the dress which sustains the phantasm (to which Lol is soon to be-

---

[2]This article first appeared in the *Cahiers Renault-Barrault, December* 1965. (TN)

come fixed) of a beyond that she cannot find the word for, this word which, as it closes the doors on the three of them, might have espoused her at the moment her lover was to raise up the woman's black dress to unveil her nakedness. Will this go further? Yes, to this unspeakable nakedness that insinuates itself into the place of her own body. There everything stops.

Is this not enough to reveal to us what has happened to Lol, and what it says about love; that is, about this image, an image of the self in which the other dresses you and in which you are dressed, and which, when you are robbed of it, lets you be just what underneath? What is left to be said about that evening, Lol, in all your passion of nineteen years, so taken with your dress which wore your nakedness, giving it its brilliance?

What you are left with, then, is what they said about you when you were a child, that you were never all there.

But what exactly is this vacuity? It begins to take on a meaning: you were, yes, for one night until dawn, when something in that place gave way, the center of attention.

What lies concealed in this locution? A center is not the same on all surfaces. Singular on a flat surface, everywhere on a sphere, on a more complex surface it can produce an odd knot. This last knot is ours.

Because you sense that all this has to do with an envelope having neither an inside nor an outside, and in the seam of its center every gaze turns back into your own, that these gazes are your own, which your own saturates and which, Lol, you will forever crave from every passerby. Let us follow Lol as she passes from one to the other, seizing from them this talisman which everyone is so eager to cast off: the gaze.

Every gaze will be yours, Lol, as the fascinated Jacques Hold will say to himself, for himself, ready to love "all of Lol."

There is in fact a grammar of the subject which has taken note of this stroke of genius. It will return under the pen which pointed it out to me.

You can verify it, this gaze is everywhere in the novel. And the woman of the event is easy to recognize, since Marguerite Duras has depicted her as non-gaze.

I teach that vision splits itself between the image and the

gaze, that the first model for the gaze is the stain,[3] from which is derived the radar that the splitting of the eye offers up to the scopic field.

The gaze spreads itself as a stroke on the canvas, making you lower your own gaze before the work of the painter.

Of that which requires your attention one says, "*ça vous regarde:*" this looks at you.

But rather, it is the attention of that which is regarding you that has to be obtained. For you do not know the anguish of what gazes at you without, however, regarding you.

It is this anguish that takes hold of Jacques Hold when, from the window of the cheap hotel where he awaits Tatiana, he discovers, stretched out at the edge of the rye field before him, Lol.

Do you read on a comic level his panicky agitation, be it violent or only dreamed, before, significantly, he gets a grip on himself, before he tells himself that Lol can probably see him. Just a little more calm, and then the next phase, when she knows that he can see her.

Still, he must show her Tatiana, propitiatory at the window, no longer moved by the fact that Tatiana hasn't noticed anything, cynical at having already sacrificed her to the law of Lol, since it is in the certainty of obeying Lol's desire that he will go through the motions with his lover, upsetting her with those words of love whose floodgates, he knows, can only be opened by the other, but these same cowardly words tell him that this is not what he wants, not for her.

Above all, do not be deceived about the locus of the gaze here. It is not Lol who looks, if only because she sees nothing. She is not the voyeur. She is realized only in what happens.

Only when Lol, with the appropriate words, elevates the gaze to the status of a pure object for the still innocent Jacques Hold is its place revealed.

"Naked, naked under her black hair," these words from the lips of Lol mark the passage of Tatiana's beauty into a function of the intolerable stain which pertains to this object.

This function is no longer compatible with the narcissistic

---

[3]For an understanding of the function of the stain in Lacan's theory of the gaze, see his "The Split between the Eye and the Gaze" in *The Four Fundamental Concepts of Psychoanalysis*, trans. Alan Sheridan, New York: Norton, 1977, pp. 67–78. (TN)

image in which the lovers try to contain their love, and Jacques Hold immediately feels the effects of this.

From that moment on, in their dedication to realizing Lol's phantasm, they will be less and less themselves.

What is manifest in Jacques Hold, his division of the subject, will no longer concern us here. We are interested rather in how he fits into this threefold being, in which Lol is suspended, laying over his emptiness the "I think" of a bad dream which makes up the content of the book. But in so doing, he contents himself with giving her a consciousness of being that is sustained outside of herself, in Tatiana.

It is Lol, however, who puts together this threefold being. And it is because the "thought" of Jacques Hold comes to haunt Lol too insistently at the end of the novel, when he accompanies her on a pilgrimage to the scene of the event, that Lol goes mad.

The episode in fact contains signs of this, but I would point out that I heard this from Marguerite Duras.

The last sentence of the novel, which brings Lol back to the rye field, seems to me to bring about a much less decisive end than my remark would suggest. One suspects from it a caution against the pathos of understanding. Lol is not to be understood, she is not to be saved from ravishment.

Even more superfluous is my own commentary on what Marguerite Duras has done in giving a discursive existence to her creature.

For the very thought, by means of which I would restore to her a knowledge which was always hers, could never encumber her with the consciousness of being an object, since she has already recuperated this object through her art.

This is the meaning of sublimation, something that still confounds psychoanalysts because, in handing down the term to them, Freud's mouth remained sewn shut.

His only warning was that the satisfaction it brings should not be considered illusory.

But clearly he didn't speak out loudly enough since, thanks to them, the public remains persuaded to the contrary. And the public will remain so if the psychoanalysts don't come around to acknowledging that sublimation is to be measured by the number of copies sold for the author.

127

This leads us to the ethics of psychoanalysis, a topic which, in my seminar, produced a schism within the unsteady ranks of the audience.

In front of everyone, however, I confessed one day that throughout the entire year my hand had been held in some invisible place by another Marguerite, Marguerite of the *Heptameron*.[4] It is not without consequence that I find here this coincidence of names.

It seems quite natural to me to find in Marguerite Duras that severe and militant charity that animates the stories of Marguerite d'Angoulême, when they can be read free from those prejudices which are intended solely to screen us off from their locus of truth.

This is the idea of the "gallant" story. In a masterful work, Lucien Febvre has tried to expose the trap it sets.

I would draw attention to the fact that Marguerite Duras has received from her readers a striking and unanimous affirmation of this strange way of loving: of that particular way of loving which the character—whom I placed not in the role of narrator but of subject—brings as an offering to Lol, the third person indeed, but far from being the excluded third.

I am delighted to see this proof that the serious still have some rights after four centuries in which the novel feigned sentimentality, firstly to pervert the techniques of the convention of courtly love into a mere fictional account, and then to cover up the losses incurred—losses parried by the convention of courtly love—as it developed into the novel of marital promiscuity.

And the style which you adopt, Marguerite Duras, throughout your Heptameron, might well have paved the way for the great historian I mentioned earlier to attempt to understand some of these stories for what they really are: true stories.

But sociological reflections on the many changing moods of life's pain are but little when compared to the relationship that the structure of desire, which is always of the Other, has with the object that causes it.

---

[4]Marguerite d'Angoulême (1492-1549), author of the *Heptameron*, published posthumously in 1558-59. The seventy-two tales of the *Heptameron*, told by a group of travelers delayed by a flood on their return from a Pyrenean spa, illustrate the triumph of virtue and honor. (TN)

Take the exemplary tale in Book X of Amador, who is not a choir boy. Devoted even unto death to a love which, for all its impossibility, is in no way Platonic, he sees his own enigma all the more clearly by not viewing it in terms of the ideal of the Victorian happy ending.

For the point at which the gaze turns back into beauty, as I have described it, is the threshold between-two-deaths, a place I have defined, and which is not merely what those who are far removed from it might think: it is the place of misery.

It seems to me, Marguerite Duras, from what I know of your work, that your characters are to be found gravitating around this place, and you have situated them in a world familiar to us in order to show that the noble women and gentlemen of ancient pageantry are everywhere, and they are just as valiant in their quests; and should they be caught in the thorns of an uncontrollable love, towards that stain, celestial nocturne, of a being offered up to the mercy of all . . . , at half past ten on a summer's evening.

You probably couldn't come to the aid of your creations, new Marguerite, bearing a myth of the personal soul. But does not the rather hopeless charity with which you animate them proceed from the faith which you have in such abundance, as you celebrate the taciturn wedding of an empty life with an indescribable object.

Translated by Peter Connor

DESTROY
Maurice Blanchot

Destroy: it fell to a book (is it a "book"? a "film"? the interval between the two?) to give us this word like an unknown word, offered by a completely different language of which it is the promise, a language that perhaps has only this one word to say.[1] But to hear it is difficult for us who are still part of the old world. And, hearing it, we still hear ourselves, our need for security, our assumed self-possession, our petty dislikes, our lasting resentments. Destroy is then, at best, the consolation of despair, a *watchword* which merely appeases the menace of time in us.

How can we hear it without using vocabularies that knowledge, and moreover a legitimate knowledge, puts at our disposal? Let us say calmly, one must love in order to destroy, and one who could destroy by a pure movement of love would not wound, would not destroy, but only give, bestowing an infinite emptiness where the word destroy becomes a non-privative, non-positive, neutral word which bears neutral desire. *Destroy.*

It is only a murmur. Not a unique term glorified by its unity, but a word that is multiplied in a rarified space and by someone who pronounces it anonymously, the figure of a young woman who comes from a place without horizons, from ageless youth, from a youth that makes her very old or too young to appear as only young. Thus the Greeks hailed in each adolescent the expectation of an oracular word.

To *destroy:* how it echoes—softly, tenderly, absolutely. A word—an infinitive marked by the infinite—without a subject; a work—destruction—which is accomplished by the word itself. Nothing but our knowledge can recapture it, especially if it awaits the possibilities of action. It is like a brightness in the heart, an unexpected secret. It is confided to us so that finally, destroying itself, it destroys us for a future forever separated from all that is present.

---

[1] I refer to the book *Détruire, dit-elle (Destroy, She Said)* by Marguerite Duras.

130

Characters? Yes, they assume the position of characters, of men, women, and shadows, and yet they are immobile *points of singularity*, although a course of movement through a rarefied space—in the sense that almost nothing can happen there—is traced from one to another, a multilinear course along which these immobile points never cease to change places and, finding themselves identical, to change. A rarefied space rendered infinite by the effect of rarity, up to the limit which nonetheless doesn't limit it.

Assuredly, what is happening there happens in a place we can name: a hotel, a park and, beyond, the forest. Let's not interpret. It is a place in the world, our world; we have all lived there. Still, while open on all sides by nature, it is strictly delimited and even closed: sacred in the ancient sense, separate. There, it seems, before the action of the book or the film's interrogation begins, that death—a certain way of dying—has done its work, has introduced a mortal inertia. Everything there is empty, missing, in relation to the things of our society: missing, in regard to the events that seem to occur there—meals, games, feelings, language, books that are not written, are not read, and even nights which belong, in their intensity, to an already defunct passion. Nothing is comfortable because nothing in this place can be completely real or unreal, as if writing staged, against a fascinating background of absence, only the semblance of phrases, residues of language, imitations of thought, simulations of being. Presence unsustained by any presence, be it yet-to-come or in the past—a forgetting that supposes nothing forgotten, and which is detached from all memory, without certainties. Ever. A word, a single word, last or first, intervenes there with all the discrete brilliance of an utterance borne by the gods: *destroy*. And here we recapture the second requirement of this new word, because if one must love in order to destroy, one must also, before destroying, be liberated from everything—from ourselves, from living possibilities, and also from dead and mortal things—by death itself. To die, to love: only then will we be able to approach that fundamental destruction, one that an alien truth destines for us (as neutral as it is desirable, as violent as it is distant from all aggressive powers).

Where do they come from? Who are they? Certainly beings like ourselves; there are no others in this world. But, if fact, beings

131

already radically destroyed (hence, the allusion to Judaism); yet, in such a way that far from leaving unhappy scars, this erosion, this devastation or infinite movement toward death, which lives in them as their only memory of themselves (in one, as the flash of lightning which finally reveals an absence; in another, as a slow, unfinished progression of time; and, in the girl, through her youth, because she is fully destroyed by her absolute relationship to youth), these things liberated them through gentleness, for attention to others, for a non-possessive, unspecified, unlimited love, liberated them for all this and for the singular word that they each carry, having received it from the youngest, the young woman of the night, the one who, alone, can "say" it with perfect truth: *destroy, she said.*

Sometimes, they evoke mysteriously what the gods have been for the ancient Greeks—always on an equal footing with them, as familiar as they are alien, as close as they are far away. New gods, free from all divinity, still and always to come, although descended from the most ancient past; men then, but relieved of human weight, of human truth, but not of desire nor of madness, which are not human traits. Gods, perhaps, in their multiple singularity, in their imperceptible duality, that rapport of themselves with the name of night, oblivion, and the shared simplicity of eros and thanatos—death and desire finally within our reach. Yes, gods, but, according to the unsolved enigma of Dionysus, mad gods; and it is a kind of divine exchange that, before the last laugh, in the absolute innocence to which we must accede, leads them to designate their youthful companion as the one who is mad in essence, mad beyond all knowledge of madness (the same figure perhaps that Nietschze, from the depths of his own insanity, called Ariadne).

Leucate, Leucade, the brightness of the word "destroy," this word that shines but doesn't enlighten, even under the empty sky, always ravaged by the absence of the gods. And do not think that such a word, now that it has been pronounced for us, can belong to or be assimilated by us. If the "forest" without mystery or symbolism is nothing other than a limit impossible to transgress, yet always surpassed in its impassibility, it is from there—the place without a place, the outside—in the tumult of silence (such was Dionysus, the most tumultuous, the most silent), apart from all possible signification, that the truth of this alien word emerges. It comes to us, from the farthest point, across the great clamor of destroyed music, coming, perhaps deceptively, like the very beginning of all music. Something, sovereignty itself, disappears here, appears here, without our being able to distinguish between appearance and disappearance, nor between fear and hope, desire and death, the end and beginning of time, between the truth of the return and the madness of the return. It's not only music (beauty) that is announced as destroyed and nevertheless renascent; it is, more mysteriously, that we witness and take part in *destruction as music*. More mysteriously and more dangerously. The danger is immense; the pain will be immense. What will become of this word that destroys? We don't know. We know only that each of us must bear it, with ever after at our side the young, innocent companion, the one who gives and receives death as though eternally.

Excerpted from L'Amitié *(Gallimard).*

BIRTH OF TRAGEDY

Dionys Mascolo

Today, people who "go to the movies" (because we usually
give in to a desire to go to the cinema rather than decide to see a
particular film), have had the experience of being seized by the
suspicion, the harbinger of evidence, that the cinema could well be
a complete, irreducible, autonomous art form, capable of perfection in its genre, with something to say which neither the writer,
the painter, nor the musician is capable of saying by his own
means and which is all the more poignant as it is experienced by us,
and unknown to us, as one of our still closed-off "depths."

Here is a film that brings about this possibility. *India Song* is
a birth in filmmaking. One of its possible births, of course. But it
was Dreyer, and none other, who paved the way. A straightforward
statement. This film is important first of all in that it convinces us
that the cinema is just beginning, or rather that the time of "great
cinema" has just begun. It has emerged from limbo. Many films of
undeniable beauty, many filmmakers worthy of esteem and admi-
ration did not, however, go in the direction of this breakthrough.
As a result, we are just now at liberty, we filmgoers, to start talking
about it. From now on, we are involved, just as we have a right to
be involved in written works (ideas) or events (intervention of
needs—demands, desires, and requirements in politics) and generally speaking, everything capable of modifying the course of our
life, and not merely those things ornamental to it.

But because we are talking here about one particular film, we
have first to settle an argument with the cinema itself. Really each
of us has something to settle with cinema, that troublesome mir-
acle which, from disappointment to disappointment, has led us to
pursue with less and less faith the moment in which its promises
would be kept, what it contained of something yet-to-be having
been incessantly deferred and, at the same time, incessantly reaf-
firmed. It is a case of an unhappy love affair: we love the cinema
but have never been given a film to see.

Born from recently developed technology, subordinate from
its inception to the law of money, deprived of a history or forced,

134

in disorderly and unprecedented haste, to make itself a second-hand one from borrowings, "adaptations" and detours, in thoughtless imitation of what took thousands of years to develop, mixing all genres, periods and styles—the cinema created the monstrous museum we know. The astonishing thing is that the possibility for new beauty could awaken there, but we should realize that it is never beauty that was lacking. In the same years, out of the same spirit of limitless speculation, the incomparable architectural splendor of New York was born.

Before it was beautiful, however, to put it simply, the cinema was from the start, *stupid*. Let me qualify this crude statement. The cinema was born stupid because it was born powerful. That is its original curse. It is stupid like Power. That is, stupid twice over: like power, and like servitude in its obedience to the sheer "force of things." Its innumerable products, which have assured its domination over humanity's imagination for more than half a century, its works, and even its masterpieces, bear to different degrees the mark of that primal brutality that characterized it from the beginning. Its birth was not the birth of an art. The waiting, the infinite exploration of the darkness from which form is modelled, was not permitted in its case. Had it adhered to its one certain truth, modest to be sure, but present from its onset, it could have become a privileged means of recording documents (of life sciences, of current history: *news*). It immediately turned away from this, annexing all existing systems of writing and all their works in a gesture of overbearing imperialism whereby it set itself up as a total art form, paranoid, justifying its claim by the law of the survival of the fittest because it had at its disposal a formidable power: the image. That is, "the real world," reality, completely at the disposal of the cinema and the cinema alone: its given, its foundation, its substance, its "fortress." The image—that which does not allow itself to be discussed, authority itself. The image again: not only irrefutable, but quasi-ineffable—allowing at most a sigh of "it's like this" as earlier the view from the mountain (but isn't this natural spectacle with its vertices and ravines already like the cinema?) encapsulated all Hegelian discourse.

That isn't all. Remember that this "art," largely dependent on the progress of technology, was on this account condemned to be born twice. Deprived of a history or constrained by an unbearable acceleration of its historical time, it had, nonetheless, a pre-history, its silent period. This prehistory had already produced its Lascaux (Eisenstein, Chaplin), when the impact of which new technology, once again, is capable, produced an interruption in its growth, then a regression, or an advance that some believe to have been fatal—the talkies. Double birth, double immaturity. The cinema never recovered from this trauma. Even today, it betrays its silent origins, up to and especially in its most elaborate, least "prehistoric" forms, precisely because it is still trying to get rid of them. Hence the truly barbaric poverty of a kind of dialogue that began with the talkies, and the unspeakable ineptitude of what is called "movie music," no less awkwardly symbolic beneath its expressive exterior than simplistic circus music.

The love of cinema, called *cinephilia* when it is intentionally cultivated, is not without shame. This is the most common experience: some incredibly lazy film contains a sublime sequence. These flashes of genius shine only as the reward for those with courage enough to plunge into the empty hell of what's been seen a thousand times. A strange endeavor. And the key to the film-lover's disorganized state, beginning with his need for delirious self-justification and, resulting from that, his use of a very exaggeratedly noble and intellectual language. But delirious justification aside, we are all like that. Underlying our love of the cinema are just such moments of involuntary poetry. So the film-lover's memory, its museum, contains very few works. It is really an anthology, a collection of fragments and vestiges, of quotes, as is said in reference to texts, or of details, with regard to canvases. But this choice is never acknowledged. The "sublime sequence" is usually extended to the entire film. Esthetic cinephilia becomes the ideological obstacle which, added to others, opposes all development, progress, and emancipation of the cinema. It is conservative, obscurantist, retrograde. And, from the opposite direction, so is the spirit of "scientific research" applied to an art where the human element plays so large a part. What does the humanistic scholar do with a work that doesn't lend itself to the process of reduction which is his goal (whether it be the "means of production" or "the return of the repressed")? What does he do with a work that discourages determining truth from falsity, this truth that lies precisely in the fact that it is false (that it reveals the overwhelming presence of the false), mendacious, illusory, or as I have said here, "stupid"?

But perhaps these questions (and with them many others they evoke or presuppose) are already completely formulated in a unique and remarkable fact of experience, a veritable syndrome that need only be interpreted correctly to clarify something of the strangeness of the cinema itself, a strangeness that until now has been rather strangely respected itself. We seem, in fact, as consumers of films, to have finally adjusted to a phenomenon that we generally consider as harmless as it is constant, a sort of discouraging minor calamity whose persistence has never ceased irritating us, but which becomes completely intolerable when we focus on it and turn it into a question. It's this: how can it be that the cinema, which, if we judge by the small amount of thought it has attracted, and counts for so little, is also the source of the most lively disagreement among those very people who, through an intellectual complicity, usually find themselves in agreement on the most serious, "biggest" issues. Principles and tastes, exigencies and judgments are useless here, are suspended: they no longer apply. What regions of our inmost doubt must it touch to be like that? Why is the cinema, and soon cinema alone, impossible to talk about, as if it destroyed all possibility of a common language, while we have such language at our disposal for other kinds of discourse, including politics? Because unspoken, could the cinema be something we have not yet thought about? We don't know where to begin. Why haven't we succeeded yet? Not only would the cinema be experienced in a shame we might share, but also, more definitely, in a secrecy that can't be shared, that is everywhere rejected, beyond all law, each of us alone with it every time.

Is this saying too much? Hypotheses, questions, and non-answers emerge naturally from what is in question here. As to the loss or decomposition of all common language, to what quasi-psychotic interior experience would the cinema be capable of leading us? Or might it be that this ghost of a total art—precisely because it has succeeded many times, with such violence and by surprise, in melding into one the faculties which act separately in us—might finally deprive us of our habitual resources, plunging us into a disarray more soothing than auspicious, as does the simplest of our dreams? Might that be it? To stop there would be to

137

entertain the current illusion that I intend to contest. Cinema can neither be looked at nor treated as a second kind of sleep, which it also is. And, in any case, if it is a dream, if it is something of a technique for producing dreams, since the dream exists in its entirety in the least important and most realistic films, we have to say that from now on there are dreams and dreams. A total cinema, the idea of which we experience already, is infinitely beyond works that serve the "real world," even when they are subservient to the realism of a dream. There is something missing in total cinema, but it is also "in the air," so close sometimes that it is palpable, about to give birth to a declared need. But we won't be able to satisfy this need unless we become, in rather large numbers, critical of our dreams as well. The film-lover should no longer flatly admire the oneiric character of the cinema, just as the filmmaker should not crudely exploit it. For when "cinematographic" and "oneiric" are almost synonymous in everyday language, we are no longer saying or doing anything. This oneiric character, taken as the real point of departure, cannot in itself be the goal. It is, on the contrary, by starting out from cinematic material (the image) defined as the *"real world inasmuch as it is only accessible to the filmmaker as already and necessarily having an oneiric form* that cinematographic work can give birth to works creative not only of "beauty," but also of critical analysis, of a negativity and destructive power that do not work to the detriment of the dream such as it might be constructed in the work. Rather, a completely new lucidity and skepticism would be necessary, a "superoneiric" effort capable, to begin with, of relegating the original oneiric quality to its realistic insignificance. That is what we must first reveal.

To put it briefly, it is as if the majority of those who judge cinema conspired to relegate it to the poverty of a sub-product. They glorify this poverty. Writers persuade filmmakers that they are the kinds of writers who possess an irrational magic (a depth, an ingenuity, an unconscious) and in addition a special poetic genius (all qualities that, again, boil down to the one and only reality of possessing the *image*). In response, the most cautious filmmakers finally let themselves be convinced. They become the writers of their trade, their films become "literary" films. Today's major filmmakers, those who fill the great screen of criticism and study, consider themselves failed writers and they behave accordingly (they imagine, conceive, and "create" in reference to this). Their own films are expedients in their eyes—nevertheless, they also keep waiting for something of this cinematic genius to inscribe itself in them.

This is a corruptive longing that results in the artificiality, the lack of substance and of pathos in the majority of works of "great cinema" (but not necessarily in westerns, for example, where to play in a minor key is at least to play fair). Because I must insist on this, "the cinematic unconscious," if it is also the place where "the id speaks" loudly and falsely, far from being primary, constitutes itself as unconscious only at the end of a prolonged association with all cultural products—and if we are to suppose that it is also "structured like a language," it can only be in the sense that it reroutes and absorbs into itself all other languages. In this respect, the signifiers, the symbols, the phantoms of this unconscious are dangerously close to being only reappearances (disguised, hallucinatory, or "poeticized" via the image) of all the prejudices, commonplaces, and banalities of thought, all the wisdom of a universal stupidity. All the more so because the elements of this new language are originally closer to the literary model, hence far removed from the "real functioning of thought" that a new "automatic writing" would explore, that would be formulated in a discourse that uses language "to signify something *completely different* from what it says," because it is at this point that the surrealist project and psychoanalytic research meet.

It was said that it would be first a writer, rather than those who also work in a sense on the inside, who would finally succeed in proving that cinema can be liberated from its literary decadence and endowed with a discourse of its own that can rival literary writing. But it first had to be disengaged from its primary evil, that is, it had to be divested, which meant at the same time divesting ourselves, of all the *power* that was latent in it from the beginning, in the sense defined above (the unexamined prestige of the image, the image not criticized as already "oneiric") had to rid itself of it, all the while running the risk that such a demand, at least at the beginning, can be regarded less as an opportunity for reform than as an impoverishment, pure and simple. In this work of ascesis, a whole realm of experience acquired in another domain was put to good use in a bold and forthright manner.

139

Marguerite Duras is not a writer who makes films on the side. Nor is she a writer who adapts her books so she can reduce them to film. She began in a most remarkable manner by rewriting some of her books in the manner of films. But in rewriting them in this way, she engaged in an activity which, rather than bringing them to perfection, began to requestion them instead, and attempted to exhaust them, as if she were demanding from them an impossible achievement in another dimension. Conducted with rigor, this activity brings about the destruction of the book.

To echo Rimbaud, it is cruel, terrible work. Because it didn't involve making the book say more but rather drawing from it what it could not say as a book. Nothing less than this then: to go beyond the limits of the book through film. Far from a sub-writing of literary cinema, what is at stake here is the quest for a cinematographic sur-writing. The literary model could no longer hinder the author of the films in this pursuit—that was Duras's strong point and her good fortune, because she started out as a writer who tested the limits and tried to go beyond them. I must say that she brought to the task a rare determination, but also and above all the most enigmatic energy, an extreme imprudence of which only a woman is capable, a penchant for risk taking different from the kind that heroes of the "spiritual" life have accustomed us to, and the ability to question all certainties, our acquired sense of security, in a high-stake game which seems guided only by an *inconceivable* (unable to be conceptualized) confidence in the unknown as such. Such energies could produce an unknown and specifically feminine form of the poetic imagination, of the passion to understand, of the work of thinking, if these energies were to turn away one day from the "struggle for existence" in which they have been wastefully consumed until now.

Speculating about the profound desire that compelled the author to rush headlong into such an adventure,[1] I would say it was probably the desire to give words—spoken words—their greatest power. This discourse which, in writing, is present as spoken

---

[1]There is not enough space here to retrace, as ought to be done, the itinerary followed. After *La musica*, where efforts of transformation were minimal, the dialogue, left unchanged though subjected to the modulations of a logical chain of framed images, took on a driving force. Moreover the inscription of the visible, already tragic effects of the spoken word in the film persuaded us that it was

(therefore absolutely separate from the rest of what is "written") had to be disposed of according to other laws, rules other than those governing unspoken words, allowing speech to create itself as a strictly non-transcribable event. And for that to happen, we must suppress the "remainder of the written" which incubates, prepares, and foreshadows it in the book and is given to us to understand only after it's been rendered endurable, and to replace it with something neutral relative to language, or something else non-linguistic. This could only be accomplished by the image—the ordered succession of images, and not theatrical space, which is always too encumbered even at its barest and has a presence and a depth which are too disturbing, distracting, and, in the end, too consoling. The goal was to allow the tragic world to make itself heard again, as that which should not be able to be heard. *India Song* attained this goal.

At the same time it is clear how far the destruction of the book went. A part of the text was reduced to image, the other part had to wait to be spoken essentially in the same way as the musical phrase waits to be executed. It's not surprising but, rather, illuminating that the viewing-audition of the film inversely comes closer to an active reading, a kind of decoding that engages the "viewer" in a complex, even contradictory, anxious movement, in which he himself tends to produce something of the missing book. Far from recalling the book (the knowledge of an already verified idea) of which it is the emanation, the film awakens in us an unaccustomed desire, one that must have been active from the dawn of civilization, the desire that the word which it brings—the first, virginal word, (the poetic word ascribed in other times to the gods)—be somewhere inscribed. The desire for the book. As if it were necessary from the beginning of time that once spoken, this word, in order that it not be lost after having been received into thought, had to be recorded.

In this film we are dealing not only with the first tragedy in cinema, but with the resurrection of tragedy itself. Doubtless,

---

really film, not "filmed theater" as it might have appeared. Four other films followed, but you have to go back to *Une aussi longue absence*, directed by Colpi where, more than in Resnais's earlier *Hiroshima*, with its treatment of the major theme of forgetting, the possibility of the film's going beyond the book was already taking shape.

tragedy has deserted the theatrical stage forever. Drama has driven it away, but to refer to "drama" is, in fact, to point indirectly to the novel alone, if it is true that everything written as "theater" in modern times has been written under the reign of the novel (atheistic, in essence), and in its way a "play" is only the reduction to anecdote, to psychology, or to the moral of a potential novel, a novel *brought to the stage*. In other words, deprived of the novelistic dimension in writing, it becomes a ghostly literary genre. Therefore, tragedy has been replaced to a lesser degree by drama than by the novel. Or, whatever enabled the novel to emerge made tragedy impossible. In fact, the most laudable efforts to bring tragedy back to the stage that was made for it have been in vain and will remain so as long as novels are being written. It has been said that tragedy would re-emerge elsewhere; as certain films foreshadowed, it did so on the screen.

A tragedy that is in no way Greek. It doesn't come from a pre-existing idea of the tragic that would have guided its restoration. Making a *tabula rasa* of every cultural reference, every system of thought, every religious survival, tragedy is being born here, directly under the influence of the high pressures or high temperatures of modernism, as "naturally," necessarily, and savagely as it appeared in the Greek world. The first "Greek tragedians" did not invent tragedy. They revealed the spirit of the time, that is, its expectations, its questions, its malaise. That is why the least prepared spectator—though he needs to be contemporary— can recognize himself immediately in *India Song*, which is not, strictly speaking, a spectacle.

Additionally, this modern tragedy (from which the divine is so little absent that we must see how it stages a devastating advent of the "savage God" whose oracle Yeats named for us at the beginning of the century) is all the more "modern" in our eyes because it is also without question an act of great romanticism, an eternal romanticism with few manifestations as brilliant since the romantic revolution. This proposition can irritate only those who insist on denying out of scholarly prejudice the notion that not only in everything that awakens and moves us are we in a period of romanticism, and come from it, but also that everything that takes us

142

outside ourselves, our *otherness*, everything absolutely future-oriented in us—if you will allow such an extension of the "absolutely modern" which, once a necessity, is now only a necessary condition—proceeds entirely from what it set in motion at a moment in the history of this sensibility. A proposition that becomes on reflection completely banal, if it is true that the "subject" itself in these times needs to be reinvented after having been destroyed.

Tragedy without action, one might say, or rather the celebration of a mystery. All the action in this film takes place "outside" our field of vision. We are never in the present. What takes place before our eyes admits at once to be a simulacrum. It is the commemoration of an event that occurred very long ago (nevertheless dated: Spain destroyed, the Congress of Nuremberg, the revolution betrayed). The actors don't incarnate, but only signify at a distance or symbolize the people through whom the things evoked actually happen. One shot shows Delphine Seyrig in front of the portrait of a woman long dead, whom she portrays: A.M.S. This woman is assumed from the beginning to exist somewhere apart in her full reality: as if pre-existing *in us* are all her possible figurations—more real than the living woman—benefitting from the inexhaustible richness of myth in impersonal memory. In the same way, it is useless to ask *who* maintains the cult of memory around this figure; the question admits only one answer. We do. The Indian servant who lights incense discharges our service. . . .

Thus, everything that happens on the screen is rigorously distorted and disoriented.[2] The evocation takes place at the French Embassy, a palace, already dilapidated on the outside, which one enters with the camera, only to be plunged into an interior space, a space still of the mind, of memory. What's more, the spoken words are never *seen* at the same time (never "synchronous"). The speaking subject is never in the image when he speaks; he only appears when others in their turn speak off screen, sometimes about him. Nevertheless, speech is not distant but is amplified by its closeness

---

[2] Asked to say a word on the reason for such a procedure, the author answers, "*In order not to lie.*" It is fine that such a "simple" requirement ended as such a necessity.

to inner speech—not weakened, but on the contrary, purified of all theatricality that would diminish it—like the lovers' words, detached from our view of their faces in the shadows, or like those words that can be written to someone but are impossible to utter (which is simply to write)—and that are spoken paradoxically or in an unavoidably incoherent way. To write them perhaps permits something to be said that can't be said without madness. In brief, in order to reach us the text communicated has to traverse a space that is first completely destroyed, then reconstructed in such an unfamiliar way, with such a different orientation, that it finally reaches us as a blast of sublime brazenness.[3]

Space with a different orientation, insolent boldness, these words lead us to another, *music*. This tragedy in film is constructed throughout like a musical composition. We think not only of the film's soundtrack, the importance, the richness, and the dynamics of which are so great that the image, in an unprecedented way, sometimes seems to exist just to support it. The whole film, including the images, is composed like a musical score. The images are so many staves of the score, as are the frames, the sets in which they are placed or that they keep in the background; camera movements (alternating mobility and immobility); the movements in the shot (choreographic); expressive gestures (tempo of actors directed like orchestra musicians); the music itself—musics, rather, for one is exterior, the other not; the sounds (the birds, the cosmic noise of the sea) from which all the realistic noise (steps, doors, glasses) is excluded: in this regard the film is silent; the voices, a quadruple system of unrelated words: "present" voices of the officials, the atemporal timeless voices that sometimes comment on an evoked

---

[3] In the case of a work that is as studied and as close to perfection as this one in which the slightest error might even be taken as intentional, it is my duty to point out the following negligible imperfections: (1) The shot in which the nude bust of a young man seems to announce a slightly dubious vein of eroticism that the film does not explore (the most erotic image in this profoundly chaste film is a man's hand stroking a bicycle handle). (2) The two times when the actors in the image, mute as usual, let us understand at the same time what "they" (the characters they represent) had said (because the whole story is in the pluperfect). A present on the verge of being constituted at this point, the tragic spell is about to be broken. But perhaps it involves something besides an error, a limit reached in a game begun. The rule that sets it up threatens to turn against it (once unveiled, to withdraw, destroying it).

event over the image in the manner of a recitative whose incantations allow continual passage through time barriers, sometimes "meditating" on the action; finally the present-absent beggar woman's voice—eternal because it represents the innocence and unhappiness that always prevail in the world. The whole central part of the film ("the reception") is a series of entrances, exits, questions, responses, looks and gestures, of recollections and premonitions, music and cries, all calculated with astonishing coldness, making an incurable knowledge of things rise like the sea, in an overwhelming assault, stamped with the mortal serenity that connects certain passes of the muleta. It is certainly the death sentence, final and complete, of hope itself.

The Vice-Consul (M. Lonsdale) is Thanatos: an irresistible appellant. He cries out his desire for absolute pleasure, inconsolable in his heart of hearts because he knows he is condemned to live within limits. A. M. Stretter is the Queen, surrounded by mannequins, her lovers, one of whom is her accomplice, the pivot of a merry-go-round of desire. Her plenitude lies in wait; sickness devours her, inner music and intelligence exhaust her. The summons that doesn't summon, doesn't summon her, that asks nothing—a dazzling answer to her desire—overwhelms her, bringing her waiting to an end.

The annunciation is made up of a suffocatingly dense dialogue, in which every word—the angel here speaks again insistently, like a "hammer speaks"—destroys one dimension, opening another. In a few sentences, the old world we lived has exploded. Revealed to us at this moment is the mystical wedding of the man-virgin of Lahore and the queen, at first in the closeness of an understanding in which injunctions between the two alone are exchanged as if in silence; and then, immeasurably amplified in the unleashing of a madly premeditated fury, in which thought itself grows until bestial with the force of cataclysm, sparing nothing, sweeping away the feckless lovers and all the temple facades in a coupling that distance makes truly titanic: Eros and Thanatos united. It was howled—it had to be almost unbearable like the absolute "yes" which ends the crescendo of the last act of *Wozzeck*. Afterwards, a long time into the night the man-virgin's panicky voice that hangs over the city returns to strike, to penetrate the queen who is immolated a thousand times. The farewell and the final caress will be reserved for roses which can, more than the mannequins of love, redeem the ancient world rather than abandon it, condemned.

Only a vacuous human race survives the obliteration of the individual, the one who "hunts in the warm waters of the Delta," the singing idiocy of a neolithic humanity[4] brought back to the truth of its origins, before illusion, before the great wandering of civilization that will end up in a search after reasons to live. At this point, in submitting to cosmos-chaos—cosmos turned into a chaotic falseness—no remedy, no outcome, no hope is admissible. Only a new innocence, perhaps . . . . But as there has never been innocence, it can't be called new. There is nothing to wait for; or, only the signs that would announce the coming of an *irresponsible* humanity. Mutation. The "ancient mystery" which is *India Song*, what is astonishing in it (saying ancientness from the point of modernity at which we are now) has obvious appeal.

The consequences of such a film and its value as an example are incalculable. I'll restrict myself to these points: (1) It allows us to imagine how certain unorthodox stories (those by Maurice Blanchot, for example) can become films without becoming impoverished, if the adaptation can play on their different possibilities or orchestration by displacing and redistributing the various levels of writing, allowing speech to enter like royalty, leaving the image to express part of the text in silence (for example, "it was snowing"). Before this film, the cinema clearly lacked the means for such audacity; (2) Similarly, the audacity to look seriously for an answer to Eisenstein's dream was lacking, that is, to show at work on the screen theoretical reflection itself, or the passion of thought which is, however, eminently representable because it is essentially in exigencies and "dramatic" refusals that it always ends. The time has come for the cinema to cure itself of its stupid tyranny and its timidity, which have had their day and must be swept out together.

---

[4] "Humanity was perhaps wrong in going beyond the neolithic," Alfred Metraux said superbly.

BETWEEN THE VOICES AND THE IMAGE
Pierre Fédida

The voices and the image.

Write, she says. This writing is woman's body. All and Nothing. It is exactly here that writing comes—between an amnesiac text born of a voice which is sustained by the single repetition of a gesture, and the film of images, the recollection of which is always checked by memory itself.

Destroy, she says. The image can only exist immemorially, and its violence comes from that single moment of its apparition which arrests the fascination for the absent figure. The man, perhaps. Surely, the woman.

Each spectator is thus empowered, as in solitaire, to be his own narrator, of a story—his own story—which he shall never know. Marguerite Duras's writing gives birth to a strange speech; speech which moves in that inner zone of silence where the power of hearing is *spoken* and where voices can intrude upon the echoes of fragmented words. What we have come to call *characters*, roles or expressions, are the projected figurations—always intensely instantaneous—of these echoing voices which carry fragments of speech. The voices do not accompany the visual image: they provoke it, sometimes only to abandon it like a wreck; or, again, they encounter the image to shatter it and also to draw it out to its most extreme *jouissance*—a kind of orgasm which makes it swoon.

This fainting is the expiration or stranding of the body when the voice has reached its limit and when, along with the voice, the silence of an inner space, guardian of the shadow and mark of the absent one, has disappeared. Thus writing would be a wholly external scene, violent bodies acted upon: the madman is a writing whose shadow has disappeared. Extreme writing, drunk from knowing or interpreting too much; madness haunts writing, which to be possible always has to be sustained by the silence in which it originates. The text—Marguerite Duras's text—assigns to silence the power of a place of inner speech, charm and terror at once. This speech is terrifying because no narrative can contain it nor prevent its shiftings nor even guarantee a boundary to what is

147

opened up by it and in it. Can man stay on his feet only because of what he tells himself?

There is movement even in immobility. Immobility moves to the rhythm of the characters in their doings and undoings. Rhythm which coexists with style is the interior time of writing: it is nothing other than the time of inner space—in a word, writing itself. Is this what one would call a slowing down? No. The relation of immobility to movement is essential in the constitution of appearance in such a way that appearance makes the body *the event*. Marguerite Duras's writing creates the space where the body finds the one essential truth which allows the body to speak of itself finally as real: immobility is an infinitely sensitive surface and what acts upon it is nothing other than gesture. This gesture cannot be expression: it is inscription.

Is this body a man's or a woman's? One would be tempted to say that this is a question raised only in order to identify bodies once one has gathered together their scattered debris, uncovered in freight cars. Does memory have the power to reassemble the debris which amnesia covers over by an infinite repetition of this at once past and present scene, a scene in which the body of the lover is both male and female? The scene is the *epic gesture* of the body: no difference whatsoever between the sexes can be determined in it. The *primal* scene, one might say, beyond all memory and caught up in an infinite repetition: she is still back there, at the window of an anonymous hotel room. She is back *there* because she has never stopped being *here*, in this body with its own desires.

Perhaps there is only one body, and this body represents the golden number of love's unique encounter. It demands pure beauty. It is the event itself. It has all the fragility of the event, as if what it shows were made for that one gaze which can hear and touch. Bodies destroy each other by the insistent revelation of their sex: Marguerite Duras's writing provides the body with an immemorial place which is nothing other than the presence of the time spent with the absent one. This event could be called adolescence.

If not, then the woman lover is just a woman, and the man a kind of system of montages and equipment in the form of theories, reasonings, endless explanations and nameless projects. Within the concept to which he is confined by the cultivation of his own presumptuousness, man has become like the prophetic god of whom Freud spoke, armed with an omnipotent speech which would claim to guarantee an ordered world and which believes itself the repository of absolute knowledge. Such a man has lost his adolescence. He has lost love because he no longer carries within him the power of absence. He is as though driven mad by his own reason. Destroy, she says. Indeed, nothing about him can be written: his "actions" make him merely the narrator of his sex, due to an overvalued affirmation which misunderstands the negative.

Writing—exactly like *analuein*—is a work of unbinding. We have said: this writing solicits, provokes or engenders the internal interval of a formidable silence where words move, borne on the echoes of voices. This silence is a theater of anguished shadows. It is the *sign* of the absent one. This silence which engages the terrifying immobility of the body is positioned in that place of "lack" which psychoanalysts have called a *void* which discourse pretends not to know, in order that it might not hear itself in what it says. This silence haunts discourse, which continually flees it. And the discourse or the action are sometimes composed of the illusion that they can fill in this void, or that this void does not exist. Without the film of voices, the film of images would only be sustained by the projected illusion of an action capable of filling up the void. The voices could not accompany the images nor provide a commentary on them. These voices—called "women's voices"— "come from a nocturnal space, as though from above, from a balcony above the void, above everything." "They come near to the image, then set off for a white perimeter, where they become diluted and die without a trace. Ceaselessly. Women's voices. Crossing and circulating, they flow through the body of the film, wed it, drown it in their flesh, cover it up, die of it." Thus the images are in no way helped by the voices in the space where the two meet: the voices flood in endlessly—before disappearing—and disorient the images, disturbing and leading them astray. Marguerite Duras's writing—between voice and image—carries this unbinding to the extreme limit, and this limit marks the end of that certitude of objective representation which had stood guard over a space set in place by man—for his gaze, his thought, his speech and his actions—in order to master his anguish. The fetishization of the nude female body and the enterprise of representing sex rests on a truly hallucinatory denial which can certainly be understood in terms of castration but which would take into account the visual destiny of the object and its space as they are present in the image, present for a gaze which hears nothing. A gaze, in sum, which solicits a compulsion to speak once more only when a blind spot can be glimpsed in it. And yet, literally, there is for man something unheard of in the sight of a nude. The imagery of women's liberation is sometimes caught in the trap of a bodily and sexual liberation sustained by the lure of being able to show what was hidden: the gaze of man is its entrapment. But if there is a terror that can seize man to the point of destroying him it is rather a terror provoked by the woman's discourse at that moment where this discourse makes heard a voice whose power *uncovers* this defect. The female sex represents allegorically this defect that man wonders about, viewing it projectively without anything ever being said about it, because castration cannot take place anywhere but in discourse itself, in the interval of silence where it can be heard.

Paradoxically, the film of voices produces this interval of silence where the images of sight can no longer hold.

At the moment when memory no longer engages what there is to be told, repetition is possible. And also madness—not just any madness—woman's madness, or that of childhood, or of adolescence.

Man is a commercial traveler. And all theoretical discourse can resemble a commercial traveler's when man is made up of rational arguments. Women welcome this man and with all their silence they listen to him and hear the childhood in him. They listen to him with a look and a gesture whose slowness or immobile movement do violence to his discourse. This discourse succeeds in being silent. It yields to the meanderings of a space where only music or voice can indicate that it is the immobile place of a strange violence.

Translated by Peter Connor

HOW SHE WORKS
Benoît Jaquot

M.D., who has read a lot, reads very little today. Her horizon is not, is no longer, our library, but the shelf she has added to it and now promises to set ablaze, from book to film, as it grows longer. Since *The Ravishing of Lol Stein* she has played a game with a limited hand at her disposal, a minimal "signifying battery," with which she tests or risks the different possible combinations. In his article "A Child is Being Beaten," Freud describes the fantasy as a simple sentence (subject, verb, direct object) in which all combinations can occur around an irreducible invariant (the verb). M.D.'s books and films work more or less on this model, with their circulation of obsessively repeated names, the musical clash of an exterior Far East with an innermost, hidden, West—"Judaic." For M.D., the invariant consists of a blank, something unsaid, an "absence-word, a hole-word, whose center would have been hollowed out into a hole, a kind of hole into which all other words would have been buried. . . ." It is only on this basis, I believe, that it is really possible to talk about what she does (with few exceptions, this has scarcely been done). It's a little like Sade's boudoir, therefore, where names refer to places, to bodies of men and women (sometimes the same name refers to a man and a woman: Stein), forming a distinct figure, called book, scenario. The shape falls into place; it's filmed, it's written; the facade is dropped and the book, the film is finished.

The custom in current productions is to prepare the film for two or three months, to film it in the same amount of time, taking a little longer to edit it, almost a year in all. The rest follows the first hiatus; producing a M.D. film takes no more than two months. One morning she called me to help her with *Nathalie Granger;* two weeks later shooting began, and two weeks after that it was finished. Although more difficult (it was very cold) the filming of *La femme du Gange* went along at the same speed. To demand so little time implies restricted choices. You do this because you can't do that; that will be done another time, in another situation. This intense condensation of the conventional amount of time is a preliminary requirement for M.D. Once the "big picture" is set, she needs everyone to be in a rush—technicians, actors, herself—which, necessarily, disturbs the division of labor, very well defined in a film crew. She is the last person to be deceived about the allegedly inconsequential relation between a film's production method and its reality as a finished product. It is crisis-making as much as filmmaking that M.D. practices, for herself, the actors, the technicians and the system.

M.D. never wrote a shooting script, at least not until *India Song* (the script of *Nathalie Granger* published in *Ça* no. 1 was worked out after montage). There is, on the one hand, her text, book, or scenario; on the other, the technical code, the cinematic rhetoric. Two styles, rather two languages, whose most violent collision she guarantees by refusing to undertake the translation of one into the other. We find in that principled position, which consists of not wanting to know anything about "technique," a strength of denial similar to the one that runs through her films. She writes her scenario without paying attention to the so-called "possible" or "impossible" of omnipotent technology. (There is an analogy between her relationship to technology and what she sets up between the film and the spectator, always ultimately presumed to be male; mastery with its back to the wall, defiance ceaselessly renewed, power held in check.) So we see at the center of each film crew a recurrent nucleus made up of the same names (script girl, camera man, assistant). They shuttle back and forth, put together the translation and bring back to her the indispensable scraps that she reuses immediately somewhere else. In their first days, new arrivals encounter—in spite of these intermediaries—the most uncanny strangeness, their "know-how" disintegrating rapidly on a sort of Rosetta stone covered with moving hieroglyphics. The rapidity imposed on habitual activities accelerates the rhythm of questions which, by overlapping, end up forming a ground on which one moves to the beat of the ongoing project. Importance of M.D.'s voice: principal instrument of seduction constantly used to attract those who surround her to the figures she weaves. A voice that specifies, comments, questions with a gentle insistence that commands a response.

From its beginnings, the cinema's dominant representation is that of a body in pieces, divided into parts. The actors (the *ac*-

tresses) lend their names to a pair of breasts, legs, buttocks, thrown on the market to fill a demand, variously programmed according to fashion. Since the sixties, along with an increased psychologizing of motive in fiction, we have witnessed a displacement upwards that fetishizes the face, the gaze, and the voice—and a sublimation of the fetishism inherent in the instituted code, with porn serving as an outlet. To sell one's body for money as a reproducible object, unconditionally guilty (to be an actor, *actress* of the cinema), implies a basic complicity with the organizing grid of clichés. From this, perhaps, comes M.D.'s predilection for stage actors—what she gives them to do in her films disrupts routine attitudes on the set. Following the example of others (for instance, the Eisenstein of *Ivan the Terrible*, Dreyer, Mizoguchi), she does not think of the actor as radiating interiority, as a repository of fetishes, but as a silhouette signifying in his relation to the frame in which he is set and in relation to the text that he intersects. In general, she makes her actors rehearse together before the filming. Their first acquaintance with M.D.'s direction is as disconcerting for them as it is for the technicians: non-existent or rare close-ups, the use of off-screen voices for the customary dialogue, the length and immobility of the shots. A sort of Duras troupe exists which seems to keep growing: D. Seyrig, C. Sellars, N. Hiss, J. Moreau, M. Lonsdale, G. Depardieu, D. Mascolo. Knowledge is implicitly transmitted by one or the other to their uninitiated partners—who, surely because of M.D.'s mischievousness, often play the role of intruders—and this has a bearing on what their *function* will be: the calligraphy of bodies on a beach, in hallway or a room, a slow choreography inscribing the reiterated terms of the same desire.

In M.D.'s films the critical moment involves a central place around which everything comes to a head; the search for it is the first object of the preparatory work when it does not indeed precede the concept for the scenario: the hotel room in *La musica*, the houses in *Destroy She Said, Jaune le soleil*, and *Nathalie Granger*, the deserted luxury hotel in *La femme du Gange*, the exotic drawing room of *India Song*. Unlike Sartre's *huis clos* which contain or enclose, these are what M.D. calls "echo-chambers," the off-screen space assuming as much importance as what the camera lets us see (least). Once this place is found M.D. goes there frequently to identify what she calls the "filmed perimeters." She cuts the

153

space into slices (the angles of the shots), reconstructing it according to a logic that punishes conventional naturalism.

To ask, among other things, if this critical moment is the cause of the lengthy, stationary shots or if the reverse is true is the same as asking the question about the chicken and the egg. The accelerated rhythm of her direction brings with it a blurring of hierarchies (writing, filming, editing). M.D.'s method is not linear, the way a film is usually produced; writing is simultaneous with editing, shooting with writing, etc.

We must admire the reflex-exactness of the idea that M.D. has of her place in the system. She is little interested, or only in a vague way, in the destiny of her work at the sociological level. Her approach aims for the close questioning of a subject, the opposite of addressing a massive audience. If she knows this or that person has acknowledged her, she wants to see, hear or read him or her, those who vicariously represent for a moment all who follow her, one by one, or even anticipate her, watching for her films. As for the possibility of a commercial success, it must be understood that she is always certain of the worst. In contrast to her status as a writer—a "star" of the biggest publishing house in France, whose books are published as soon as written, distributed, bought, no matter how difficult—M.D. is, in a sense, completely extrinsic to the film industry. There, her name has no such exchange value, she doesn't earn any revenue from this activity (not since the time she first began directing). The producer disburses a sum of money (an advance, generally small, from box office receipts or from television). M.D. does not want to risk anything at all for an enterprise she originates (she is reconciled to this situation which she does not try to change). Most often the technicians are paid, the workers always, of course. Given her single-set locations and the reduced time of filming, the (small) estimate is never exceeded nor does the film go into a deficit. She is satisfied with a room and a few showings every day so that those who wish may attend them. Her films are supernumerary objects, *de trop;* they roam the perifery of contemporary film production, and sometimes irritate it.

To write about the production of *India Song* is to inventory differences, account for misfortune. M.D.'s films have been made, until now, with an almost euphoric facility as if carried along by an irresistible urgency. This time M.D. received a higher than usual advance on receipts (Fr 250,000), but too little for a costly production (the rental of sets, costumes, etc.) and complex shots which required more time, thus more money. The hurried filming, instead of being imposed by the movement of the film itself, resulted strictly from economic necessity. The advance on projected receipts for *Nathalie Granger* was provided in March 1972; by the end of April the filming was over. *India Song's* advance, paid September 1973, meant that the film couldn't be finished until the end of June 1974. A chain of accidents during these eight months brought M.D. to the point where, with the shooting imminent, she hadn't the least desire to go through with it; administrative annoyances prevented the release of funds; the actress who was supposed to play the role of Anne-Marie Stretter suddenly refused to do it for unclear reasons; the actor who was supposed to play Michael Richardson claimed huge expenses, which made his taking part in it absurd, etc. At the last moment—which in a roundabout way reestablished the order of things—M.D. chose Delphine Seyrig and Claude Mann (he had never worked with M.D.); Michael Lonsdale, Matthieu Carrière, Didier Flamand, Vernon Dobtcheff already having been engaged for a long time. With the filming deferred from week to week, M.D. rewrote her shooting script compulsively (while before this she had never written one at all) and found herself on the set confronting a multiplicity of possibilities instead of a single solution which had been the case before. Hesitations, incomprehensions.

The first day, before beginning, the full crew was previewing routine tests. With no definition, and a set of defective lenses, they had to put off working until the next day, using other equipment in exchange. Then there was a shakiness in the image (they noticed it during the first projection of the rushes). Finally there were entire sequences, the most difficult and the most precious footage, that burned in the laboratory. Two extra days (guaranteed by the insurance) were needed to re-do them. Bataille's remark: "How can one linger over books (films-B. J.) to which the author has not noticeably been *compelled*," a remark that could be understood in reference to M.D., takes on unforeseen meaning in the light of the situation. The astonishing thing (which says a lot about M.D.) is that once past the threshold of the unendurable, the curse stimulated her (curse: what is said badly, cannot become discourse), she repaired what seemed ruined, made the best of disaster, and finished without further drama the editing of the one film which, from what I have seen of it, goes furthest on the path she herself opened up.

August 1974

PATHS
Joël Farges

La femme du Gange introduces a fertile division that Marguerite Duras will carry to its highest point in *India Song*, both a film of images and a film of voices. Inseparable but distinct, the same film and yet different; each cutting a singular passageway through the narrative flow, a most unique crossing. One with the other, one against the other ... a new and prolific divergence whose character is to exhaust representation. A crisis that alerts us to or, rather, alarms us about what representation could mean.

Here is the traveler: an enigma (at a crossroads, cut adrift from three novels: *The Ravishing of Lol Stein, The Vice-Consul, L'amour*)—this enigma is centered, it advances, slows, scatters, loses its way, would find it again perhaps if the boundaries didn't happen to be missing.

Incidents: an accident we're told about or are made to see its tardy echo, its prolonged reverberations. Tensions without visible conflict, words that are unmotivated but overloaded with meaning, a zone of the unsaid brought to life, an interrogative movement of bodies in the frozen immobility of the whole: real undecidability. For you, the active, frenzied work with this undecidability itself. Unexplored until then, paths to an infinite and unprecedented film-text.

A space of listening, space of a gaze crossed by emptiness, swept away by relationships, exchanges, complications, approaches: they touch, the better to circulate, to break up. An interval (should correspond directly to Vertov's) that establishes the text-sound (where is it? absent like the larynx that makes it vibrate . . .). An interval that establishes an anaglyphic volume of perception, open to illimitable readings.

In this play outside the film frame, the image loses its power, abandons its despotism, is decimated by the incendiary incantation. The set immobility of the image takes on something of the plot construction in a scene that never comes, never really reaches its end. These fixed images lose their power all the more because they are full of color. Applied in spots, in uneven traces (because the film was damaged), the strong dominants of the shot used: ultramarine, flesh-color, black of the dress material ("black spot"), yellow-gray of the sand that forms a "certain image," vitreous green of sea. The color (or more aptly, the ink) suppresses realistic effects and makes an imprint of the film's rhythm.

These voices lift a strange veil. Here a woman sees her lover slip away. At the ball that is evoked, people talk of other things, yet no one really talks. These two voices (the eyes are closed) have a clandestine knowledge kept fresh in an eighteen-year old's memory, but what they say is alien to our inquiry, ever unsatisfied. One of them forgets sometimes, the other rushes to assist; here is an unstable, incomplete, fragmented knowledge that does not acknowledge us.

This place of transmission, these conditions of listening ("They talk to each other. They are unaware of the spectator's presence.") show that they speak only for themselves. An imaginary posture, in trompe-l'oeil, because in fact it is for us—envious witnesses of their languor: desire and death—that they whisper, becoming seed to be scattered to the winds of mortal desire. Confidences overheard, purloined, stolen away unbeknownst to them as they flow out toward death.

Voices of women. Voices without a plan or place except, perhaps, one that is nocturnal, opaque, black as night, transparent and dangerous. Disembodied voices, whose circulating flow abandons to our hidden listening a few threads of desire that animate and extinguish them. Voices that explore what they see, what they feel will happen deep in their bones as they wander and intersect one another.

"See them," say the voices. Voices without eyes, blind voices, but voices that scrutinize.

These voices, what are they? Without bodies, nobody's voices. At the edge of the music, invisible. It's *La femme du Gange* that goes beyond the impossibility of seeing the voices. What these voices emit and utter, in their physicality, is profoundly material; this is the paradox. Body of voices without bodies, breath drawn into the lung, feminization of timbre, shuddering of dentals, hissing of the lips, slight sounds in the throat and palate, fragile immanence of the tongue—in short, a whole "stereophonic of the flesh." Through the remote scratch of the microphone, a different body rises up, made of pieces of organs, eroticized parts of bodies.

Voices without visible bodies, there nevertheless, present in the signifiers, in the pulsating beat of events.

Waiting for death for so long, for every death, for all of history, what do these twin voices do? They join together, merge without a trace, without a place, nowhere. Kindred spirits and sisters in a room, of which we see only the half-opened crack in the door inside the blockhouse hotel. A predictable entanglement that kills them in return. "I love you more than anything in the world." "If I asked you, would you agree to kill me?"

In the incessant ebb and flow of the vow and the question that echo feebly in the deadly silence, the film comes to an end. Mortal desire stumbles, passing through the virtuality of bodies. Those who—from every aspect absolute, immovable, stones in mid-current—are prey to desire are pledged to misfortune or to die serenely as if waking from sleep, shrouded in secret silence, mute.

L.V.S., emblem of matriculation: her still voice, her life suspended, her solitary perspective, what else?

The beggar woman who passes, on the contrary, has a body, a hungry body, but she does not hear the cries she utters. She has no voice, or only a deaf voice.

The voice that burns is dead. I don't understand. What is a dead voice? A discrete but tenacious passage through the body.

But a voice or an inflection are always ephemeral. Always quick to be extinguished, to die. To want to restore them, keep them alive, is illusory. "To make them live" means "see them dead."

This murmuring of the two voices is punctuated by resonant constellations—squalls, undertow, swells, pounding, beating waves and winds that rise alongside still scenes in which phantoms pass. Benumbed and troubled silhouettes of characters who are immobilized and look at residues of evaporated scenes and who lie in feverish expectation of a muffled shock or a tragic song that might turn everything upside down. (It comes, this sad song, from the woman in the middle of overturned, faded, dead flowers. With her mouth completely closed, she allows her throat to vibrate, *blue moon.*)

Still images: a shot of a strange group only intermittently representable. A system of representation frustrated by discontinuities, by immense, oblique or crooked frames, and by moving voices.

Here is the traveler; he doesn't look at anything. Doesn't see. Why has the traveler come? To see the place where they loved each other. Blind, he doesn't see the rest.

The others—always the same—remnants of a broken community, avoid the blockhouse hotel which like the forest is a limit, a barrier, a boundary marker, a provisional zone that cannot be penetrated or violated. Always outside, always alien, they are afraid. They survey the space. They look. They look at it. Gazes and silent listening, and everywhere a telescoping of the scopic and appellant. We watch them look, see them see. A powerful trajectory of eyes passes through bodies and through walls. Emergence of voices in the corner of an eye which has her attention, an eye which captures, which seeks to ravish. A strange play of gazes fills the film.

In what might this film's economy lie? With this dispersion, this narrowing of margins, combined with the film image and the sound track, *La femme du Gange* creates a space, an always inalienable and unlimited mass in which the production of meaning consists in always beginning again as the same and different, endlessly and forever.

La femme du Gange. A complete but divided film. The role of the two voices, off to the side, is to express the written text, uttered outside absent bodies, in broken inflections, suspended intonations with a loss of voice that ends things, "emotive" muteness, work on *tessitura*. Against this, we have still shots, caesurae imposed on features of the representation, slow fragmentation, gestural activity in strange slow motion. In one direction, and in another, are new paths that have no end.

Writing and image, dissociated from one another, establish this incessant stereophonics, made of tangles and snags, harmonies, whirlpools and echoes in which the inundated reader is forever cast adrift.

An empty place, a fission or a signature of things torn, a discontinuous interlacing: I pass through it, articulate it, set it free, journey in it.

160

TERRITORIES OF THE CRY
Viviane Forrester

Forget memory. So slow, this world where flowers fade, and the stones. *India Song* destroys the distance where time insinuates itself. Anne-Marie Stretter—"she is in the past," Marguerite Duras told me one day, "she has this grace." A reign without bounds, without hope of boundaries (death itself doesn't make the least difference any more) in this place, the space of the screen where the worst things live undefined, uncategorized, outside language. Here is life in its simplicity, where incurable beauty and love refer back, like hunger, to pure unendurable presence, where mirrors do nothing but replicate. Sun, mirrors, lamps in the shadows, and flowers—like the original apple is anodyne and like these roses in whose recesses a vegetal, exhausted Delphine Seyrig is shipwrecked, in an instant—reveal more about this ultimate story where nothing can end because it has already ended. We haven't left paradise. That was it—eternity, the horror. The Vice-Consul knows it. The sublime beauty in Marguerite Duras reveals it, and the terrible sweetness that engulfed Anne-Marie Stretter, surrounded by her lovers. Nothing touches her. Michael Richardson's hand, so tender, at night, on her hair, is useless. Useless, his embrace, their embraces. They are resigned to it, to love and ecstasy that lead to nothing else, transgress nothing. All those things that Duras's books touched, that they challenged and demonstrated through the most translucent indications suddenly appeared naked, erasing what made a palimpsest: the identity between the signifier and the signified. It seems that here the signifier, splintered into diverse media, each of them autonomous (image, sound, space, continuity, direction), cancels itself out, and that being springs forth, at last.

Now, what always underlies Duras's work, and life, what History has tried from its beginning to suppress, what cannot be said *or* proposed *or* heard (but which film permits, we find, in its flexibility, its clarity, its dynamic simultaneities) can break out: the cry. Something forbidden, a major interdiction.

The Vice-Consul's cry. Forever and ever heard by Anne-

161

Marie Stretter, by Marguerite Duras, and held back by the man from Lahore. This howling is the language that truly belongs to the earth and its inhabitants. A response. There is no other. Discourse, even speech and music itself exist to distract us from it. This time we hear it. It spreads, opens out. We see the distance it covers. And by seeing it, we hear it.

The Vice-Consul and Anne-Marie Stretter are the same, always separated, fused in this separation. They speak as they dance at the French Embassy. So as to say nothing, to say that there is nothing. Nothing to say. That they know. And he (Michaël Lonsdale) whose unforgettable gaze at the lovers by the Ganges at the beginning of the film held the most unbearable knowledge, he—the subject of scandal, locus of love, the one they are going to send away—announces that he is going to cry out. He is going to display his brute suffering, the demented knowledge he has of it, the state he incarnates: understanding. And it is here that the cry reaches its source. The primal source. The man who was all gaze is going to become voice, a sound that was inaudible until now, the only sound in the world.

And we hear a cry. We hear it said, proclaimed, that someone loves. We hear what has never ceased. Anne-Marie Stretter—erect, calm, innocent—dances, frozen in this cry that she has never stopped crying out in silence. Over which the music that she loves and fears sometimes makes a screen (or a passageway?). Motionless, next to the equally motionless man, she accepts, submits, acknowledges. The cry comes like falling rain. It is everywhere, outside the screen. It absorbs dimensions, space; it surrounds, disperses, meanders. Lonsdale's voice becomes geographic. An opera. Everything is stripped to the most obscene purity. A territory without shame. The name of Anna-Maria Guardi is scattered, linked to the music that Anne-Marie Stretter, under her maiden name, had played earlier in Venice, far from any embassies. The cry of a name. Name of the cry. Rocked by the swelling of a paroxysm that could conceivably create love. But no one is shouting. Scarcely a sound. Nevertheless, the cry is there, inextinguishable. And so we think of Marguerite Duras who must hear it all the time and know that she hears it, who seeks and flees from it. Here the screen becomes the concrete space of what she calls the crisis of writing.

The man, the woman are still standing, forever motionless, navigating, navigated. Then a gesture, a man's hand moves slowly toward the bare skin of a shoulder. That's all. That still exists. Nothing else is possible. In the late hours, the Vice-Consul moves away. It's on the morning lane that the vibrations of the cry still reverberate. The world of dawn, pale echo of the terrible expanse on which the Vice-Consul's silhouette, seen from the back, disappears from view once again. He walks in rags, the same ones he's been wearing since Lahore (where he shot at lepers and dogs in the Shalimar gardens, and at himself, in the mirror, at home). Slowly the silence settles in again, identical with the shouting from now on.

Still echoing intermittently in the embassy drawing rooms is the name Anna-Maria Guardi, now once more Anne-Marie Stretter, who regains her body and the body of the other—desire—with a wounded smile. The cry is extinguished as the beggar woman's song is reborn, a natural sound like the song of a bird, poignant in its ignorance, rejoining in its utter misery the Vice-Consul's impassioned act. Cries of fishermen, of workers, raucous cries of birds, the world creates itself anew, covers over the scandalous uproar. The rest will follow; the story and the impossible ending of the story are inscribed there. Some signs, roses, the effigy of a life and that map of the Indies at the end, flesh of the world, inscribed in a certain silence that the cry will sign.

"OUTSIDE TURBULENCE"

François Barat

"It is an incessant, very hollow gnawing away, beyond time and measure." —L'amour

In despair hope. For so long we have awaited the collapse of these class societies: but it's coming through, drawing near, beginning to surface, making waves: because it's here, in the films (on the films!), so it's elsewhere, that is, in a revolutionary elsewhere. Because then, here, elsewhere, over there, yes! place of a major statement, place of popular memory, living stones in the people's struggle, individuals in the trials of love, because then, mouths shut tight, silent. THEY sing. THEY sing, THEY sweep, cook, mop, get screwed, make babies, iron, reheat, polish, repaint, repair, yes, THEY sing.

A body moves (at first) imperceptibly, gently sways varies bends. Movement of bowed head as the music sweetly swerves. Song and music arrive from the hidden depths of this place of loss, this moment of madness, from afar. Then it flows there it goes everywhere what's to be done.

Doll's songs, songs miraculously saved, miniatures and frescoes, despair, cries of light, mad loves, burnings inside, skin that sheds, falls.

Inverted images which restore hearing, grant a hearing, words groaned. Piano at chocolate time, little songs for birds still warm and dead, held in the hollow of the hand. A child, at the foot of the tree, the sea, I dig a first grave and everywhere there are violins, no doubt, the make-up of the dead invades me. Because in your films THEY hum; that woman, sitting right on the ground, beside what. Music of pursed suffering, seized at the end of a body that breaks, shows pain, mauve meaning. I know already (in history) this kind of brief song of love, of separation, of rupture. Evoke! arms around neck, close to mummy's skin: the song comes from the throat, from the breast (for the child awake, asleep, half enfolded in its niche) I listen then to these songs coming from you, from your history and from your splintered, scattered tenderness, recalled, revived and replayed from your childhood. We spoke of a young woman glimpsed among the tombs at Père Lachaise, in the immobility of an infinite truth of suffering, collapsed, shattered, crushed, trampled, naked, ridiculed, tortured, denied. Where it sings, in what harshness of the body do these opaque, obscure notes lodge, vault, resonance and liberated desire, liberty, liberated words, reheard, returned, reconquered, revolt.

And the body of the film shudders under the violence of the tightened mouth, or the violently gently raised mouth of the beggar woman who casts her song over the whole Ensemble, over and beyond everything, into the void, the elsewhere, our hole, return to the center, like the railing which guards the sea, which dances alone *in the middle,* encircling the silence in her arms, tender movement of the shoulders; up to there this song! up to this shore of soft singing which is to say of what remains, a painful holding back. Listen, somewhere, a voice, a body, over what is it weeping?

One day I'm crazy in my kitchen. I am humming "When the lilac blossoms, my love, when the lilac blossoms forever." Around the refrain, fleeting turbulence, dances in the squares, dance music, fires, sirens, explosions, bombs, the devouring throng elsewhere, trying to invade our organs with its glue. The throng, the turbulence, causing an uproar, the sound effects and sound track of a tragic moment, the foreign menace, the imperialist steamroller, the end of regional identities, the death of the subject, the dialectic of stupidity, of emptiness, of a death which brings, modern Attila, nothing.

> Change your mind
> and it is the sign thus so pointed . . .
> of LOVE

Change your mind. Today, the twenty-fifth of September, nineteen seventy-five, over what else is this woman collapsed around me crying, over whom these sobs, over what that is identifiable, over what story beginning where, if we had no more tears, over whom these sobs, these blood clots which are red humid violent.

Echo forever returned, chain of central moaning, chain of central cry. That's enough. Today THEY cry over five men assassinated by Spanish fascists. There also reason sinks in terror ever since we have been living in anguish, when shall we live in hope?

> "It is a slow march with solemn strains. A slow dance, for funeral balls, for bloody festivities. She does not move. She listens far away. She says: —I must sleep or I'll die."

Change your mind, and or change the record and let everything drift step forget step forget popular memory, songs, motets, madrigals, laments, songs for the dead of the revolution, selective memory, it must sing everywhere, standing, the cries, whispers, let us strain our voices to let the hollow be heard, our territory, silent, an elsewhere which circumvents seeps inward.

> "He says:
> — Silence begins with the spaces opened between times.
> The moaning has just opened.
> —Look."

Translated by Peter Connor

MARGUERITE AT THE SPINNING WHEEL OR GALLANT INDIA

Bernard Emmanuel Graciet

Titles nothing but balustrades in trompe l'oeil of a balcony overlooking an empty sea balls bouncing across deserted tennis courts seaside ballets for a summer ball over there in far off India perhaps or even here on this beach of silence shadow and sun away from the same and the other at the overture of the score of a sotto voce opera that will have been sung before the overture and will have taken place afterwards with this muted grace where everything is engulfed in an inexhaustible silence born from anger and murder from India's horror under the wing of the islands and as if in trompe-voice.

THE TURMOIL SCATTERING FROM HER

already in the enraped lustral on shores of laughter accomplices at a ball which will certainly have taken place swept away on folded wings tulle so black lived irrevocably she here sex ceded woven lace of ancient weave skeletal sombre light strewn raw song of her face scarcely open sketched in the fault of her desire rushing faultful cinderella lazy in the bed of the dormant letter that elides over a sororal seaside litany veil v-notched violently Lol headed toward the creases of a choreographic text inclines incurves unfolded crease of the eyelid agony lightly blinking vacillicit split into two on the beach the horror where they were re-engraved in pas de deux or more they cracked the night highwire walker of ink anciently new holing an incalculable arena of words set down at once erased by the mordant wave of noctural memory washed by dawn at the multiplying moment of Lol's madness inscribed on her dance program outside the first rendezvous perhaps again the last words at her birthday dance crossing the empty floor of a beat broken open body of a modern adolescent smiling awkwardly annulling her emblems two motionless L's fixed at the crest of her swaying hips to climb the deserted dais of the municipal casino under a thousand eyes magic in their absence lost redrowned swarming off in living losses in loping away always and again far from her link lol la lol pale firefly of a moment at that femmous ball among all those summer people where interminably played out in a fuckerring mirage will be the mad stigmata of a sterile pressure in her shielding body split iridescent bubble from a childhood sowing time at a poignant party where her former betrothal was abruptly broken off before lol dolores dolorcitos dolorous rosaried soror dolorosa ancillary sower of her unfulfilled body's ripe seeds infinitely sowing the pebbles of her subject germinated from death out of pleasuring the time of annual celebrations annulled in the pure ring of a seaside text where will have madly danced too much the young titulary leaf rod in the night wind indefinitely written in punctuation in three scarlet signs over a white abyss two proud wings in mid-flight fluttering above the water unfolding their blood-woven feathers near the gaping initial anchored in the deepest hollow of the lofting wave this ink at a child's waking will have come from a seagull sowing descri(v)ing itself above the deserted ocean.

THE OTHER SHORE

Did she come back from Tahla or Thala but had she ever left this lol valerie stein soil wandering off from a summer ball stone or tennis courts where a ball bounces in memory shimmering sea she hopping on one foot along the somber strand slender in childhood word wiles everything that is to say nothing shakes lassitude from her gentleness always to mother begun again inexorably infinite undertow of her vaguely vague attraction lol v loved by the oracle amazed maddened by the mortal fault the letter V dead L wedged in aquamarine unset not encircling the indiscernable but rather bestowing a ring tightening the knot at her constricting throat or perhaps the girl at bay changed course the flaw the blue where already settles in the mad bed on their arenaloss beach of savage night the subject of her in flight literally raised up for the ban of the other for ten years lol rising drowsily washes in the sleeping wood she turns from Tatiana on tiptoes as if a child were sleeping everything kept close by her glass slipper forgotten in her hurried exit from a ball in the sterile season through which she will have gone on sowing syllabees from her sleepy sex broken further back seaside stasis of S. Thala story hers and another the same days yet later on quickly following the trail which is erased under her frightened steps an ancient elsewhere she undoubtedly lived at the folded verge of her absent vulva the space of a ball at night at a brothel by the sea secretly in a pale fold glazed gaze that capsizes undoes the germinant dawn blink of an eye yesterday's blue desire forever lostlasting unduring in a durassian stratum superimposing orestes reborn fugitive silent irreversible inverted like the crack in a crystal glass unalterably interposed brother on a violated threshold earth bound ground curled silenced with your several weeks' account sown to the 4 winds vents V vitriol vacation value that values voice listening to voices of forbidden memory white ways of the city where she flutters a broken wing in her wake solely solar magnatine enraptured leafing the ravishing ophelian marguerite perhaps playing loves me loves me not by beaches quiet beside the water the rest frozen forgotten field of bleeding rye spewed stain that spreads stagnant mummy uncertain on the shores of the lorelei legend why not the other she the childhood friend following her faithful lady-in-waiting too knew everything about the night of the ball perceptive alert playmates said the schoolgirls a confidante who dances with her in the empty schoolyard gulf grotto grate sister gone away after yesterday doesn't lose a word never forgets tidal waves monsoon menses she would have wanted to travel you are beautiful so are you emission-memory go Tatiana go they dance does she share this desire this evening again she looked her gaze in the huge room when Lol told of her life you remember her gaze darkened vellum of her eyes of dead bones of dead seas where the incessant final and funereal ballet of the waves of her desire waltzes in mourning hard on this nothing which flees exhausted by its own bewilderment as it nears its illusory home her look silts up nothing never if not a sweet madness some Ophelia already written in the sands of a text on the next Ganges with its rustling foam sown in quiet pain in danger of clouding over in the twilight of a child's letter before she departs but to rejoin what residence what residue I did not seek to know it and where moreover does she graft her steps how does she traverse the murmuring texts of the undertow raised from the sea or the rye in the evening wind bellied around her body the sandy screens that break through with their rutting cries the gulls of the open sea engrave these texts on the silence the sky hollowed out by lost voices

STILL NOWHERE ELSE

Lol born from the end genetrice of the beginning without end of primoridal drives leaping with feet together through the hoop of the annulling page shattered emigré centenary of her youth still waiting at T. Beach or no matter where what happened over there that summer evening at the ball dark night of another age eclipse of Lol by Lol and in the same gesture of embrace there's no one who will have a place here on this beach pale petal dotted with drops of ancient ink punctuating with their long stops near and far true and mendacious the long crazed calvary of this face so sweet no one would of course have come to the rendezvous drowned in the sweetness of an endless childhood that floats on the face of the flesh she comes back to these indestructible places which will become even at this moment those of an advent hers and his and ours where the whole text will be played in memoriam Lol V. Stein in ruins S. Tahla and T. Beach like a sand castle or a house of cards she restsrains empty the page turn it reverse it memory before memory pure future madness from the past from what's written where nothing happens at the casino no further play the gambling rooms are deserted straight ahead step by step she approaches the monumental scene where everything has been shrouded pavane for a dead infanta no trace of a tomb only she resists again a long time ago as seaside dawn goes down the cry of a mute woman who doesn't stop dying of famine here comes the end of the piece here we are anorexic and famished fellow guests at the same endless end of Lol V. Stein mocking her extravagant gesture in the pernicious orient of words that could have been otherwise what's left for us but to stay here tonight to dream as she dreams of waves dream of waves to another legendary time crazy about her a thousand times in love inflamed spent on the strand of marshes flooded by swollen seas weaving thousands of times everywhere elsewhere the cloth of the coastline the scallop of the sky's rim over the blue bed open to the lip and litter of desire still for the other by chance white standard of lovers on their maiden voyage

... but now she tells about nights on the beach still fresh with naked footprints tranquil reliefs and reefs stranded we know not where

WITH LOL'S THREAD

In common of course the same vice she born an alter he or vice versa the text scans their successive returns to the banks of the Ganges alongside the river flows rolling to the end of life its waters rush and turn their course shifting directions turn by turn islands follow him in the ablative in the guise of a preamble in the neighboring place so he will play his part in Lahore moved by what climes under what colors renewed rounds in posts by turns Chandernagor T. Beach she too had traversed the ball fugitively like him this forsaken grace the folding of a dead bird clothed in black thinness only later much much later did they know that this desired skeleton was named Anne-Marie Stretter and that nothing else could happen to her but him hunger after she swept away with her non-gaze the ball she hauled here along the ashy banks of the Ganges her idle steps burdened with years with that time with the mad lovers sleeping their couple in single file that dawn over there outside it was summer without stopping Lol followed them with her eyes across the gardens when she didn't see them any longer she fell to the ground fainted perverse she must always be thinking the same thing Michael Richardson everything beginning again always the eternal triangle of that seaside moment absence-word hole-word hollowed at its center into a hole abyss of the grave vast wave without end reverberating gong void ganges impossible deserted tennis courts hole of flesh to flesh bloody arena the unfinished wave sex consummated at the turning of the tongue the threat of the tower with a hole parallels breaking through there beyond the vice-kingdom hourglass through the window-pane out of which the sea flows and the Indian sands the eternity of a ball in the cinema of Lol V. Stein Anne-Marie Stretter incognito (inconsulables) in a Far Eastern port setting sail for priests to lift ink or at dawn dear afflicted ones both with the same malady nothing more bodies bared in vain annihilated in ocelot velvet rocked uprooted by a Cardomones' wind at the hatchway with silenced voices their faces at the prow cleaving the prairie of the deep sea adrift on echoing echoes through equinoxial tides to the rendezvous in the gardens of the Calcutta embassy whose vast rooms are those of a summer casino at a seaside resort in France or rooms in Shalimar palm trees leprosy and twilight unless it is the tennis courts emptied by the summer monsoons or emptied but does it much matter

ISLANDS AND WINGS

Everything is always played in the faint light of dawn at dusk in the morning on time but where to begin go along the Ganges go up the Mekong pace up and down the shore at T. Beach plough all India don't try everything gets mired in the leprous bed which inaugurates every scene even in its consumption in any case it's that way I'm sure it's a matter of seeing into the exile called text ambassador lagoon of the gaze dance aflutter through the so pale oleander leaves during the dog days of a summer monsoon harvested palm trees splayed out in panting Indian mouths hungering growling crowded in rows or circles on awakening tears for the ambassadress of hungering to death for sounding armies of men she of the delta gangue huge embouchure flowing through virgin forest slowly dawn breaks through with leprous fingers funereal toccata in the forsaken orient that becomes its boredom sultana ind/solent we wait for her to cry it out he will not have heard Schubert played in the empty hall after the reception he will never know that musical moment or lieder idly strummed we must write them a tomb engrave on it an epitaph rest blue palm trees stein stone again to weave thalassa halo hilarious Lahore Jean-Marc of H already leaning with his elbows on the balcony balustrade at his residence all of a sudden in dressing gown waiting outside his gongs waiting his eternal attachment true affection it all depends on frail asthma which marks the day with breathless gasp on the dais at the ball of daylight wailed weaning his voice wheezing in the gape of the wound plagiarist step by step accompaniment of Blue Moon you know the famous tune he aims he rises from bed Galling India in tender erection towards the impossible secret of his delirious preference on the threshold of his delinquency in the hollow of burning sex for the first time fogged with heat intercede for me the look of the Ganges beyond such a wait and then there is nothing more perhaps to imitate if it is not a temptation or a try for the other side

172

the other image she lived in Lahore he crossed the ballroom what
do they hear now the same melody Schubert Marguerite at the
spinning wheel for instance Indiana's Song whistled by someone in
the gardens Blue Moon played on the piano in a nightclub or again
the song of Savannakhet sound of Battambang the cries of the lepers how can one know nothing more happens between them vice
reigns words without issue nothing green ocean bitter bays you
were absent from the rendezvous exiled behind park fences at the
embassy where the Queen of Calcutta's fans are turning the fences
around the deserted tennis courts the huge fence at the Prince of
Wales Hotel erected against beggars fence to keep out the sharks in
a white circle where you are not inscribed in the evening air by the
edge of the sea in a white dress cruising whirlwind she approaches
him from afar but bushes rustle with the sound of their steps unfinished sentences hints of a sweet Italian inflection no doubt infinitely evoked on the rim of the text's bottomless pit endless pa-
rade of the string of names indefinitely scanned which bring
nothing back but their own widowhood among their numbers wea-
ry burned out dislocated obscene useless to insist on the translucid
shadow of girls nymphs in rags destitute somewhere between Siam
Cambodia Burma in a market square above all the youngest thinks
she sees swimming naked in the thread of the Ganges the Calcutta
night song of a song to lose one's breath gangrene wholehearted
cries rotten with hunger needy beggar in rags annihilated by insa-
tiable gnawing desire will it stay here long change song at his side
there would be no one else only this one woman Anne-Marie
Stretter book sleep famished yawning oyster Indian sloop Venetian
gondola gliding adrift in his gaze palm tree fan seaweed from the
sea gone so soon already glimpsed foreclosed in the scent of citron-
ella closed with a stolen kiss or to stay over there in her sweet near-
ness if she wants it soon though breaking into tears in Venice
where she meets him by chance no she does not dream a cold wind
hisses in gusts that morning tap of her steps on the icy pavement of
lagoon-like streets white chalky face unknown Vice-Consul of Lahore puts in the pale wheat of masked memory confetti from the
carnival ball funereal madness asea it's as if he or she cried out as
yet in silence on that island or this flight of steps bordered with
mangoes of flesh and feather on this blinded blurred face turned
toward the throbbing voice of the woman from Savannakhet on

the other side of the island the opposite shore reclining stretched out in the shade remains there chosen one who chooses he felt passion for a woman as if it were the first time to smile broken that bathing time the virgin body defracted at sunset on the ridge of thrilling waves breaststroke flowing swimming asleep perhaps to finally cross the flooded delta on each wave exile of desire burned in tears imploring him perspiring it's so hot this shaken night plaintive angel bound in the open sea there orestes bathed in spray a wing sailing towards the islands drenched to the bone with filthy brown mud forever smiling terrifying his face streaming with sweat rare moments swimming with difficulty on the surface skimming night in Idumaea solar emergences solitary bodies sweating blood and water garnered in shadowy chambers that sleep there or there by her side here on the river bank in the lacunae heap of wings at most that slow drift knights entwined forever on the sands of the Ganges.

UNDERTOW OF THE GAZE

Swarming away in sorrow crunching sands underfoot the deep blue laceration of palm trees violets of the storm the rusty sun rising gray naked lapis lazuli the burning cry shouted to heaven at the bottom nests of tanned wrinkles fear reigns there through heavy weather there was a voice winnowing memory raw body straining in light with caressing eyelashes embarked far back aboard a building hotel steamer ship sloop dinghy junk above all strewn with insular tears at the consulate of the ambassador's wife whose missionary eyes pale at the end of unsettled night anointed with ocean oil shuddering with swells he would have liked to cleave but could not cross alone in the large gondola galley Charles Rossett's invitation to the islands he wants to know her gaze does not leave them saved from crime it's a lie you will see he throws his glass which breaks into bits and pieces death over Lahore abandoned by djinns the tomb of Djehan-Guir with its first court made of marble for maharajahs its second with clay walls where they waited in motionless rows for vultures to come from the tower of silence . . . enclosure for lepers had she lived here in Lahore in Kashmir near Shalimar he stayed there on the balcony looking out beyond the historic gardens black marble pavilions the heronries an immense and commonplace orchard in the bronze red amaranth fields vegetal ruins of a phantom park a sentimental colloquy to Gallant India moslem jade stairway palace of the rosy stone wind organ a woman with rosy cheeks who reads swarming with grotesque masks swept away by the palms a thousand and one nights of traveling streetfairs where a hand on a shoulder pulls back leaving alluvium sacrificial offerings unreal tidal wave all of that in a fog on the Tibetan border where heavy sticky clouds stayed too late like him around the strange emptiness high consular walls eaten by lichen palisades ambassador's wives abandoned at the foot of a balcony they burn blue mist shadow linga blood enwreathed and below under monsoon clouds the Ganges with its logs absently unextinguishable in the inextricable mist and an ascetic who danced and was convulsed with laughter and a Buddhist nun crying and convulsed with hunger a live torch thin flame a parasite cast off by death floating waves invalid vilified echoes the blind Ganges.

TEXT, THEATER, FILM
Jean-Louis Libois

Any commentary can only overload or saturate (as is said of a sound track) what is given as an extremely flexible and mobile sound and visual apparatus. Here is a vacant but not empty place, since the meaning that would fill it is not far off.

Underlying what is commonly called the "quality of a work" is a scene that would not be completed by this filling-in of meaning, the kind of scene that had, until now, nourished the theater.

But first, what scene are we talking about? Surface? Volume? Sphere? Everything that the eye (the ear) designates at once as its own theater ("the only theater of the mind").

But it is also a geographic and historic place, crowded and *alive*—the heart of S. Thala, to be exact, the intersection of audial and visual blocs, a sea-shell echoing with voices that sweep along with them leprosy, desire, the city, colonialism.

In short, the history of India and of the white race—foreigners, outsiders—(the position, in fact, of the voices in relation to the story they trace).

THE PLACE WHERE TEXT, THEATER, AND FILM INTERSECT

"nothing will have taken place but the place," except, at closer look, the flowing of the Ganges—vengeance on colonialism—EXILE.

Joyce, Lenin, Brecht: exile was
a decisive moment in
their practice

DARK

On the piano, in slow tempo, a melody from between
the two wars, called "India Song"
The darkness begins to
dissipate. While very slowly the darkness
dissipates, suddenly there are voices.

Curtain: lights, sounds, voices, images. What properly belongs to the theater (to its own theater); but also music that punctuates, starts the text moving again (desire; bodies dance).

VOICE I
When one thinks of what
it was. He had . . . him . . . Michael
Richardson . . . (*Silence*) Anne-
Marie Stretter (*Silence*) . . . Lola
Valerie Stein . . . (*Silence*)

To outplay forgetting, therefore to speak. This second death (leprosy), as well, threatens to exceed representation; therefore, dialogue is excluded from this theater of words insofar as it is the place of communication, of exchange.
A text with holes in it, fluctuating, proceeding by bursts and flashes: *horror* settles in the interstices, the ghost of the spectator squeezes into them.

There was Tatiana Karl . . . and the
others . . . all the others . . . the ones from the Indies . . .
the musicians . . . those people . . . all those people . . .
and all those parties . . . those balls.

Crack—Crevice—Opening—Cut—*Streak*—Groove—Wrinkle—Trace—Scar—*Notch* (dictionary of synonyms): the place where M. Duras's theater emerges.

TRAGIC SPACE

Dialectic between what is said (voice) and what (has been) done (stage). "Such is the structure of the Greek theater: the organic alternation between the thing interrogated (action, stage, dramatic speech) and interrogating man (chorus, commentary, lyric speech)" (Barthes). The voices—like the ancient chorus—know or knew, and they form a kind of breathing or breath (rhythm) that saves the scene from a semantic overload that threatens to suffocate it.

177

On one hand there is the scene; on the other hand, the voices that talk about it. Now these voices never describe the scene. The text never tries to make scene and voice coincide, but works through sliding and skidding.

In the same way, the voices do not exhaust the scene, nor the scene-as-body, nor the impossibility for the voice to weld together its contours (such as the impossible or, more exactly, *unpleasant meeting* with the beggar woman, or with leprosy).

VOICE II
You are so young and I
love you so . . .
               Voice II, imploring
I love you more than anything in the
world.   Stop.

THE SCENE FOR VOICES—THE OTHER SCENE

Voices and scene weave a space no longer visible but readable (what's read). Where the eye as a structuring moment is excluded.

The bodies convened on the stage are the *fact* of the voices. No representation is possible; the stage is immediately situated as loss. The pale figures who move there insistently bring this to mind. The only representation is textual.

To say there is no representation possible means that there must be an end to the "mimetic stage." Because "to be in the center of the gaze"—and that is what the work of Duras is about—really means what it means, namely, the geometric place carved out by desire. And such is the real "status" of the stage. (As long as the gaze exists, there is representation, Barthes says.)

These voices can be expressive because definitively cut off from any subject. At no moment does the auditor/spectator have the impression of a body concealed *under* the voice. These bodies neither play nor live because there is no subject *behind* them to "animate" them. Nor are they quoted by someone else. Who would arrange to quote them? In fact, who would quote? (It is different with Brecht, with whom quoting bodies is the first attempt to "scour" off what is lived on stage. There, bodies are quoted; so then what ordains it? History, the class struggle, materialism.) The ques-

178

tion is, from what place are these bodies quoted? Their total autonomy, of which Duras speaks on many occasions, is to be understood then in the sense that the bodies are their own instruments.

TWO FILMS

Film presupposes that if the voices don't coincide with images, they will be relegated to off-screen space. Various uses of that off-screen space of fact can be cataloged: clearly this use is extremely rare and marks, moreover, a high moment in the narrative. The primacy that tradition has assigned to visual images over the sound track implies that all use of off-screen space is experienced as a disconnection, the effect of a rupture. It has as an anchoring point the *character:* flashbacks of voices and interior monologue. It is this hierarchization of fact that a film such as *La femme du Gange* (or others such as *Lessons of History* by Straub, or *If You Imagine Robinson* by Pollet), means to contest by having the off-screen space intervene. The film of images and the film of sound are substituted for the film as a totality.

Desire circulates from one to the other. Emphasis is placed on circulation, on process, on movement. No pregnant moments. No principal signified: the phallic as well as political Father is excluded. In this way the atopical character of the Duras Text, "this blank in the grammatical chain which would be woman," can be understood, but it would be necessary to go back for a brief look at the issue of woman and writing.

VOICE I
If I asked you,
Would you agree to kill me?
VOICE II
Yes.

THE THIRD FILM
(or what could be the film of bodies)

There is no story where the body isn't brought into play. Voices 1 and 2 burn up in the body, are engulfed by it. (Fatal experience for voice 1.) Body of one who speaks and one who writes,

179

"Yes, if one can go on a little, can say these books are painful to write, to read, and this pain ought to lead us toward a field of experimentation. Finally, I mean they are painful, painful because this is work that bears on a region perhaps not yet explored."

DESTROY, SHE SAYS

There could never be an innocent text, a plenitude of text (ending in a kind of inflating of the subject who can boast of having read everything); he who aims for this can get lost in it. There is no text but the text which engages the body.

WRITE, PERHAPS, SAYS MAX THOR

Because the other scene, as Lacan showed, includes indifferently in its field both analyst and analysand. And what the analyst witnesses is not the reconstitution of a subject under his impassive eye (instance of an exterior and "healthy" ego), but its dissolution, its loss.

At what moment then is the body of the spectator implicated? ("The voices don't address the spectator or the reader. They are totally autonomous. They speak among themselves. They don't know how to be listened to.") In the same way the eye is dispossessed of its hierarchizing function, the ear must not be the receptacle where the word is deposited. Because the Duras Text precludes the possibility for the listening (and seeing) subject to cut up the text into tableaux. In other words, to use Kristeva's remark about *H* by Sollers, "No exclusion of the eye by the ear, representation resounds, sound becomes image."

It isn't a question of just any text that would bring the reader and the auditor face to face (a pure and simple transposition of classical theatrical actor/spectator space). The text is not written to *the address of:* it doesn't trace a didactic space (not to be understood in the Brechtian sense). Speech should circulate in it, be mobile. All bodies, including those of the spectator/auditor, are at stake in the "adventure in sound."

Text, theater, film—or how to outplay representation. In other words, the stage should bear the mark of this decision: the *other stage* bears that cost. And it is in this sense that Duras's practice appeals to us. At once writer, director, producer. Destroyer. A text can stand as a text, be played or filmed, but also destroyed.

BETWEEN ON AND OFF
Catherine Weinzaepflen

La femme du Gange (The Woman of the Ganges)

Nathalie Granger enabled Marguerite Duras to make *La femme du Gange*. This is why she associates these two films when she talks about them. Her reluctance to release the second film to the public says even more, revealing a secret desire to conceal it, to keep it for herself.

In *Nathalie Granger* all the repression of daily life is emphasized in a desire for slowness. Frustrated desire fills her house, her gestures and her silences. Still, there is a possibility of satisfaction. We feel it underneath the surface, even if the author wants to expose everything that holds it in check. At the level of the image, suffocation. Calm. Behind the image, we find equally strong writing by Duras who evokes the essential without stating it—the ravages of repression. Violence.

La femme du Gange effects a break, a rupture. We plunge into those spaces concealed by coherence. Is it necessary to evoke the pain that this implies. . . . Of course, there is always resistance on the part of those who refuse to yield to this other truth.

Marguerite Duras opens up two paths for us, one in the images, and another in the sound track, both of which are perfectly autonomous and, on rare occasions, curiously merged. This raises the first doubts about coherence at the formal level.

The subject matter of the film is time. Here, once again, time in memory rejects the fallacy of coherence. The traveler comes back to the place of his past. The city is empty, deadened with grief. He wants to immobilize the present. But before dying or, rather, in order to die, he comes back to S. Thala, the city where he was young. Where Lol V. Stein went mad one evening at a ball, not having been able to bear the way a woman in black, who had only to appear, had enraptured and carried away her fiancé, Michael Richardson. The traveler from S. Thala, the one whom we see returning, is the same man who left for India to follow Anne-Marie Stretter. Mad love is the only kind of love Marguerite Duras recognizes; she admits only the essential. Now, mad love verges on death. Did Lol V. Stein die from it? Or was her end madness? It is indeed Lol V. Stein, the ageless woman, who is frozen in time on a beach in S. Thala. This woman who must sleep a lot in order not to die.

Michael Richardson's love for Anne-Marie Stretter didn't last, because in the film he will leave this woman, his wife, and his children. This other woman is the figure of coherence. She is the subject of the only scene that Marguerite Duras says is "commercial," in the sense that it is similar to the banal scenes of separation we have seen so often. The scene is one of the keys to the film precisely because of its refusal to understand what it exposes. If, despite everything, the traveler's wife feels pain when love ends, this pain will be overcome, not experienced as rupture. The sirens wailing in the city, the sounds of rupture, have soon swept it away. This woman belongs to the world of lies, and the fear that crushes her will soon bring her back to this place of perdition. There is an incompatibility between two perfectly defined spaces. The one the traveler has fled, and the one he is heading for, on the other side. The other side is the past, frozen in pain. It is also the present for those who find themselves there, measuring, like a surveyor, the periphery of their death. Lol V. Stein is not there alone. The people who are with her, those who make up with her the community of refusal, are also on the beach as if to give it dimensions from the other side. To validate it. Lol V. Stein is not a unique case. She is the exemplar of those who did not survive the ball at S. Thala.

And the table at the ball, in disarray, with broken glasses and the crumpled tablecloth entwined with the black scarf, is the only footage of the past. An agonizing image. The connection is explicit between the black scarf and the black dress. The woman who has not yet reached the beach area and who moves away from the hotel, where the traveler took shelter from the irritating glare of both sand and sea, may be Anne-Marie Stretter. If Lol V. Stein's face is immobilized from that time on, the face of the woman in black is contorted in pain.

In *L'amour*, Marguerite Duras's last book, Michael Richardson encounters the mad woman on the beach. He is in exactly the same position as in the film, but a relationship between them exists, brought about by the necessity of the past.

In *La femme du Gange* no relationship is possible any more. Their eyes never meet. Solitude overwhelms these beings who pass back and forth in front of the fixed eye of the camera. The traveler looks inward. Lol V. Stein's gaze is lost among the natural elements with which she wishes to merge. The gazes of the people on the beach are fixed on the traveler, the one who will rejoin them without seeing them, perhaps, but knowing where they are.

The scene of the people on the beach is repeated; their eyes are raised, as the viewer well knows, toward the traveler who is still somewhat sheltered by the hotel walls. Stricken by the memory of love.

Such elements constitute the first level of the film, the images.

The other level cannot be recounted. The voice we hear or, rather, the voices blended together to such an extent that we believe them to be one. Voices of women, voices of desire. At the same time as the rupture is taking place, this off-screen voice catalyzes these loves out of the past in order to concretize desire. If this past is consumed at the level of the image, it also enables the voice of desire to speak, with such force, such poignancy, that it cannot be delimited. We cannot distance ourselves from it. We're surrounded. If the gaze of the viewer can be linked to an idea, to the idea of death in particular, his body is very remote from it, overwhelmed by the voice of desire. It's a matter of purity in the voice. Past and present coexist there. The past, purified through rupture. The present, under the rule of desire.

It is really a question of life or death. To die of repression. To go on lying until the end. Or, finally to refuse a society ruled by repression. That is the path on which Marguerite Duras leads us. And on this path, those who do not stand opposed to this persistent sclerosis, cannot simply turn back with impunity.

WORKS
by Marguerite Duras

1943   *Les Impudents* (Plon)

1944   *La vie tranquille* (Plon)

1950   *Un barrage contre le pacifique* (Gallimard)
Trans. *The Sea Wall* (FS & G, 1985)
Filmed by René Clément, 1957

1952   *Le marin de Gibraltar* (Gallimard)
Trans. *The Sailor from Gibraltar* (Pantheon, 1986)
Filmed by T. Richardson, 1967

1953   *Les petites chevaux de Tarquinia* (Gallimard)
Trans. *The Little Horses from Tarquinia* (Riverrun, 1985)

1954   *Des journées entières dans les arbres* (Gallimard)
Trans. *Whole Days in the Trees* (Riverrun, 1984)
Filmed, 1976

1955   *Le square* (Gallimard)

1958   *Moderato cantabile* (Minuit)
Filmed by P. Brook, 1960

1958   *Les viaducs de la Seine-et-Oise* (Gallimard)

1959   *Hiroshima, mon amour* (Gallimard)
Trans. *Hiroshima, Mon Amour* (Grove, 1961)
Scenario for film by A. Resnais

1960   *Dix heures et demie du soir en été* (Gallimard)
Filmed by J. Dassin, 1967

1961   *Une aussi longue absence* (in collaboration with Gérard Jarlot) (Gallimard)
Filmed by Henri Colpi, 1961

1962   *L'après-midi de Monsieur Andesmas* (Gallimard)
Trans. (included in same volume) *Four Novels: The*

Afternoon of Mr. Andesmas; Ten-Thirty on a Summer Night; Moderato Cantabile; The Square (Grove, 1965)

1964   *Nuit noire, Calcutta* (Inédit)
Short film by M. Karmitz, 1964

1964   *Le ravissement de Lol V. Stein* (Gallimard)
Trans. *The Ravishing of Lol Stein* (Grove, 1966)

1965   *Théâtre I: Les eaux et forêts; Le square; La musica* (Gallimard)

1965   *Le Vice-Consul* (Gallimard)
Trans. *The Vice-Consul* (Pantheon, 1987)

1966   *La musica* (Gallimard)
Filmed, 1966

1968   *Théâtre II: Suzanne Andler; Des journées entières dans les arbres; Yes peut-être; Le Shaga; Un homme est venu me voir* (Gallimard)
Trans. (single volume) *Whole Days in the Trees* (Riverrun, 1983)

1968   *L'amante anglaise* (Gallimard)
Trans. *L'Amante Anglaise* (Pantheon, 1987)

1969   *Détruire, dit-elle* (Minuit)
Trans. *Destroy, She Said* (Grove, 1986)
Staged and filmed, 1969

1970   *Abahn Sabana David* (Gallimard)

1971   *Jaune le soleil* (Film adaptation of *Abahn Sabana David*)

1972   *L'amour* (Gallimard)

1972   *Nathalie Granger* (Gallimard)
Filmed, 1972

1973   *La femme du Gange* (Gallimard)
Filmed, 1973

1973   *Les Parleuses (with Xavière Gauthier)* (Minuit)
Trans. *Woman to Woman* (University of Nebraska, 1987)

1974   *India Song* (Gallimard)
Trans. *India Song* (Grove, 1976)
Staged and filmed, 1974

1976   *Son nom de Venise dans Calcutta désert*, film

1977   *Le Camion: entretien avec Michelle Porte* (Minuit)
        Filmed, 1977

1977   *L'eden cinéma* (Mercure de France)

1977   *Les Lieux de Marguerite Duras* (avec Michelle Porte)
        (Minuit)

1979   *Marguerite Duras* (Albatros)
        Trans. *Marguerite Duras* (City Lights Books, 1987)

1980   *L'été 80* (Minuit)

1980   *L'homme assis dans le couloir* (Minuit)

1980   *Le Navire Night; Césarée; Les mains négatives; Aurélia
        Steiner* (Mercure de Fance)
        Le Navire Night, filmed, 1978

1980   *Vera Baxter: Ou les plages de l'Atlantique* (Albatros)
        Trans. *Vera Baxter or The Atlantic Beaches* included in
        Drama Contemporary: France (PAJ, 1986)
        Filmed, 1976

1981   *Agatha* (Minuit)

1982   *L'Homme atlantique* (Minuit)

1983   *Savannah Bay* (Minuit)

1983   *La maladie de la mort* (Minuit)
        Trans. *The Malady of Death* (Grove, 1986)

1984   *L'amant* (Minuit, 1984)
        Trans. *The Lover* (Pantheon, 1985)

1984   *Outside: papiers d'un jour* (P.O.L.)
        Trans. *Outside: Selected Essays* (Beacon, 1986)

1985   *La musica deuxième* (Gallimard)

1985   *La Douleur* (P.O.L.)
        Trans. *The War* (Pantheon, 1986)

CITY LIGHTS PUBLICATIONS

Angulo, J. de. *JAIME IN TAOS*
Antler. *FACTORY*
Artaud, Antonin. *ANTHOLOGY*
Bataille, Georges. *EROTISM: DEATH & SENSUALITY*
Bataille, Georges. *STORY OF THE EYE*
Baudelaire, Charles. *INTIMATE JOURNALS*
Bowles, Paul. *A HUNDRED CAMELS IN THE COURTYARD*
Brea, Juan & Mary Low. *RED SPANISH NOTEBOOK*
Brecht, Stefan. *POEMS*
Broughton, James. *SEEING THE LIGHT*
Buckley, Lord. *HIPARAMA OF THE CLASSICS*
Buhle, Paul (ed). *FREE SPIRITS: Annals of the Insurgent Imagination*
Bukowski, Charles. *THE MOST BEAUTIFUL WOMAN IN TOWN*
Bukowski, Charles. *NOTES OF A DIRTY OLD MAN*
Bukowski, Charles. *TALES OF ORDINARY MADNESS*
Burroughs, William S. *THE BURROUGHS FILE*
Burroughs, William S. *ROOSEVELT AFTER INAUGURATION*
Burroughs, William S. & Allen Ginsberg. *THE YAGE LETTERS*
Cardenal, Ernesto. *FROM NICARAGUA WITH LOVE*
Carrington, Leonora. *THE HEARING TRUMPET*
Cassady, Neal. *THE FIRST THIRD*
CITY LIGHTS JOURNAL No. 4
CITY LIGHTS REVIEW No. 1 Ferlinghetti, Lawrence & Nancy J. Peters.
Choukri, Mohamed. *FOR BREAD ALONE*
Cornford, Adam. *ANIMATIONS*
Corso, Gregory. *GASOLINE/VESTAL LADY ON BRATTLE*
David-Neel, Alexandra. *SECRET ORAL TEACHINGS IN TIBETAN BUDDHIST SECTS*
Di Prima, Diane. *REVOLUTIONARY LETTERS*
Doolittle, Hilda (H.D.). *NOTES ON THOUGHT & VISION*
Ducornet, Rikki. *ENTERING FIRE*
Duncan, Isadora. *ISADORA SPEAKS*
Duras, Marguerite. *MARGUERITE DURAS*
Eberhardt, Isabelle. *THE OBLIVION SEEKERS*
Fenollosa, Ernest. *THE CHINESE WRITTEN CHARACTER AS A MEDIUM FOR POETRY*
Ferlinghetti, Lawrence. *LEAVES OF LIFE*
Ferlinghetti, Lawrence. *SEVEN DAYS IN NICARAGUA LIBRE*
Ferlinghetti, Lawrence. *PICTURES OF THE GONE WORLD*
Gascoyne, David. *A SHORT SURVEY OF SURREALISM*
Ginsberg, Allen. *THE FALL OF AMERICA*
Ginsberg, Allen. *HOWL AND OTHER POEMS*
Ginsberg, Allen. *INDIAN JOURNALS*
Ginsberg, Allen. *IRON HORSE*
Ginsberg, Allen. *KADDISH*
Ginsberg, Allen. *MIND BREATHS*
Ginsberg, Allen. *PLANET NEWS*
Ginsberg, Allen. *PLUTONIAN ODE.*
Ginsberg, Allen. *REALITY SANDWICHES*

Ginsberg, Allen. *SCENES ALONG THE ROAD*
Goethe, Wolfgang Johann von. *TALES FOR TRANSFORMATION*
Hayton-Keeva, Sally. *VALIANT WOMEN IN WAR & EXILE*
Herron, Don. *THE LITERARY WORLD OF SAN FRANCISCO*
    & ITS ENVIRONS
Higman, Perry (tr.). *LOVE POEMS FROM SPAIN & SPANISH AMERICA*
Kerouac, Jack. *BOOK OF DREAMS*
Kerouac, Jack. *SCATTERED POEMS*
Kovic, Ron. *AROUND THE WORLD IN EIGHT DAYS*
LaDuke, Betty. *COMPANERAS*
Lamantia, Philip. *BECOMING VISIBLE*
Lamantia, Philip. *MEADOWLARK WEST*
Lamantia, Philip. *SELECTED POEMS*
Laughlin, James. *THE MASTER OF THOSE WHO KNOW*
Laughlin, James. *SELECTED POEMS*
Lorca, Federico García. *POEM OF THE DEEP SONG*
Lowry, Malcolm. *SELECTED POEMS*
Ludlow, Fitzhugh. *THE HASHEESH EATER*
Marcelin, Philippe Thoby & Pierre Marcelin. *THE BEAST*
    OF THE HAITIAN HILLS
McDonough, Kay. *ZELDA*
Moore, Daniel. *BURNT HEART*
Mrabet, Mohammed. *THE LEMON*
Mrabet, Mohammed. *LOVE WITH A FEW HAIRS*
Mrabet, Mohammed. *M'HASHISH*
Murguia, Alejandro & Barbara Paschke (eds.). *VOLCAN*
O'Hara, Frank. *LUNCH POEMS*
Olson, Charles. *CALL ME ISHMAEL*
Orlovsky, Peter. *CLEAN ASSHOLE POEMS & SMILING*
    VEGETABLE SONGS
Pasolini, Pier Paolo. *ROMAN POEMS*
Pickard, Tom. *GUTTERSNIPE*
Plymell, Charles. *THE LAST OF THE MOCCASINS*
Poe, Edgar Allan. *THE UNKNOWN POE*
Porta, Antonio. *KISSES FROM ANOTHER DREAM*
Prevert, Jacques. *PAROLES*
Rigaud, Milo. *SECRETS OF VOODOO*
Rips, Geoffrey. *UNAMERICAN ACTIVITIES*
Rey Rosa, Rodrigo. *THE BEGGAR'S KNIFE*
Rosemont, Franklin (ed.). *SURREALISM & ITS*
    POPULAR ACCOMPLICES
Sanders, Ed. *INVESTIGATIVE POETRY*
Sawyer-Lauçanno, Christopher. *THE DESTRUCTION*
    OF THE JAGUAR
Shepard, Sam. *FOOL FOR LOVE*
Shepard, Sam. *MOTEL CHRONICLES*
Snyder, Gary. *THE OLD WAYS*
Solomon, Carl. *MISHAPS PERHAPS*
Solomon, Carl. *MORE MISHAPS*
Waldman, Anne. *FAST SPEAKING WOMAN*
Waley, Arthur. *THE NINE SONGS*
Wilson, Colin. *POETRY & MYSTICISM*